Praise for *Fantastically*

...ner, scientists a... ...ies

Shortlisted for the Sainsbury's Children's Book Awards 2021 in the Learning and Development category

"It deploys just the right amount of lovely, fascinating detail to inform and inspire." *The Guardian*

Praise for the Fantastically Great Women books

"With their playful use of speech bubbles and perspective shifts, Pankhurst's books remain significantly more engaging and inspiring than the rival *Rebel Girls*."
Imogen Russell Williams, *The Guardian*

"It's a tremendously engaging read: smart, informative, inclusive and accessible, with gorgeous, visually creative art. The tone is really joyful and it's hard to imagine any group of primary-aged children who wouldn't be inspired by these stories."
Fiona Noble, *The Bookseller*

FANTASTICALLY GREAT WOMEN

ARTISTS and their STORIES

Books by
Kate Pankhurst

Kate Pankhurst

FANTASTICALLY GREAT WOMEN

ARTISTS and their STORIES

BLOOMSBURY
CHILDREN'S BOOKS
LONDON OXFORD NEW YORK NEW DELHI SYDNEY

First published 2022 by Bloomsbury Publishing Plc
50 Bedford Square, London, WC1B 3DP
29 Earlsfort Terrace, Dublin 2, Ireland
www.bloomsbury.com

BLOOMSBURY, BLOOMSBURY CHILDREN'S BOOKS
and the Diana Logo are registered trademarks of
Bloomsbury Publishing Plc

9781526615343

Printed and bound by CPI Group (UK) Ltd, Croydon CR0 4YY

10 9 8 7 6 5 4 3 2 1

For fantastically
great Luna.

Contents

WOMEN in ART

Women are the creative geniuses behind some of the world's most daring and influential pieces of artwork. Using pencils, paintbrushes or even their bare hands, these artists tell stories that bring joy, encourage hope and inspire activism. They've shown women in the ways they deserve to be seen – and these women are not afraid to break the rules.

Over half of the world's artists are women. Yet most of the paintings and sculptures that sit proudly in museums and galleries are the works of men. **Frida Kahlo** is one of the few exceptions – do you know her? Her self-portraits are adored by

1

people everywhere, and she's considered to be one of the greatest painters of the works – and rightly so. However, people are much less likely to have come across **Emily Kame Kngwarreye**, who didn't discover painting until she was in her eighties, but went on to be the first Aboriginal woman to hold a solo show in Australia.

There are exceptional women artists all over the world – so why doesn't everyone know their names? For centuries, there were rules that stopped women from working as artists. They weren't allowed to become artist's **apprentices**, so they couldn't get proper training. Even if women learned the skills themselves, many artists' guilds, (which are a bit like exclusive clubs), wouldn't accept them as members, meaning they didn't have a licence to work legally.

There were also strict instructions about what women were allowed to show in their work. But many women rebelled. In the 1700s, **Élisabeth Louise Vigée Le Brun** turned heads when she painted women ... smiling. Critics were horrified! But Élisabeth soon became one of the most sought after portrait artists of the time, and a favourite of Queen Marie Antoinette of France.

2

A century later, **DAME LAURA KNIGHT** caused a stir when she pictured herself painting a naked woman. Laura didn't care, she wanted to show that women had the right to paint whatever they were inspired by.

These kinds of rules are based on old-fashioned stereotypes about women and how they should behave. The kind that say that women should stay at home and look after their children, rather than pursue a career. This lifestyle would never have suited **Amrita Sher-Gil**. Bold and rebellious, she spent her life travelling and meeting people, and had lots of boyfriends and girlfriends. She challenged the accepted artistic style of her native India and created one of her own.

Women have also used art as a form of protest. KÄTHE KOLLWITZ risked her life by creating art that showed the destruction of war. When the Second World War began in 1939, the Nazi Party burned lots of her work.

In the USA, **Faith Ringgold** created enormous, powerful paintings that challenged racism and **segregation**. Both women hoped their art would inspire change.

But there are still barriers in women's way. Most of the world's galleries are run by men, and women are often not given the same exhibition space and opportunities that men are.

Luckily, there are women who are determined to change that. **PEGGY GUGGENHEIM** created one of the most important collections of modern art in history, and hosted the first all-female modern art  show in 1943, featuring a few of the women you'll find in the following pages. This book tells the stories of some of the most talented female artists the world has ever seen. They lived at different times and came from many different countries and backgrounds, but they have a few things in common ...

They were imaginative, strong-minded and fearless. They never gave up on their dreams.

And not only did they change people's ideas of what makes powerful art, they transformed people's beliefs about what women can do.

Prepare to be inspired!

4

ÉLISABETH LOUISE VIGÉE LE BRUN

The ARTIST WHO changed the FACE OF PORTRAITURE

Élisabeth Louise Vigée Le Brun was born in Paris, France, in **1755**. Her father, Louis Vigée, was an **artist**, and Élisabeth shared his creative flare. As a child, she loved to draw and paint, and she imagined painting people's portraits when she grew up, just like her father.

When Élisabeth was **six**, she was sent to a school run by nuns, called a convent. She was always getting in **trouble** for drawing faces on her schoolbooks, her classmates' books and even the convent walls!

Élisabeth's teachers might have found her continuous drawing frustrating, but her father always encouraged it. When she was **eight**, she did a little sketch of a man, and her father told her it was **brilliant**.

She never forgot what her father said, and kept the drawing **all her life**.

"You will be a PAINTER, my child, if there ever was one."

Élisabeth left the convent school when she was **eleven** and came home to live with her parents. She was very happy taking art lessons from her father and drawing in his studio. Some of his artist friends gave her guidance too. But, sadly, Élisabeth's father died when she was just **twelve**, leaving the family with almost nothing to live on.

She was **determined** to follow in her father's footsteps and become a **professional artist**. However, at the time there were rules that said she couldn't become a painter's apprentice because she was a girl. But Élisabeth wasn't going to let that stop her – she would learn the skills anyway! She visited Paris' most important art galleries to **study** the masterpieces on display, and to **teach** herself their techniques. She also spent many hours with artists in their workshops, perfecting her craft.

Élisabeth officially started painting portraits for money when she was just **fifteen**. She was **remarkably skilful**, and mastered a way of capturing the personalities of her subjects. She quickly earned enough money to support her mother and brother. Ladies and gentlemen of the royal court, princes, actors and writers were all eager to sit for her portraits. She could hardly keep up with the **commissions** – it seemed as though everyone wanted Élisabeth to paint them!

ME NEXT!

Meanwhile, Élisabeth's mother had married again, but her new husband was a very **greedy** man. He took almost all of Élisabeth's earnings and kept them for himself.

There was another problem too … Élisabeth had been working as a professional artist, but she didn't belong to an **academy** or a **guild** – associations for professional artists. Because of this, at the age of **nineteen** her painting materials were **seized** and taken away.

But Élisabeth was ambitious, and eager to be recognised as a serious artist. The **Académie Royale** (Royal Academy) was the best school of art in Paris, however, it admitted very few women. So, instead, Élisabeth applied to (and quickly became a member of) the **Académie de Saint-Luc**, the city guild her father had belonged to. It wasn't as well connected as the Académie Royale, but being a member meant that Élisabeth had a **licence to paint for a living** and, by the time she was **twenty**, she was so well established that even members of the royal family wanted her to paint them. She was extremely popular, though other artists were jealous of her beauty and fame. Many of them said mean things.

She'll never get into the ROYAL ACADEMY!

She's only successful because she's PRETTY!

But everyone could see how talented she was.

Meanwhile, Élisabeth had attracted the attention of **Jean-Baptiste Pierre Le Brun**, a well known art dealer who was much older than her. When he asked her to marry him, Élisabeth hesitated at first, but eventually said yes because she was desperate to get away from her stepfather. This proved to be ...

HA, HA!

UNE GROSSE ERREUR!*

(*A big mistake!)

Jean-Baptiste was a gambler who had spent all his own money, and, just like her stepfather, he took everything Élisabeth earned.

Two years later, in **1778**, Élisabeth was offered a commission that would change her life. She was invited to paint **Marie Antoinette**, the Queen of France.

Marie Antoinette was an Austrian princess who had married the heir to the French throne, **Louis-Auguste**, in **1770**, when she was only **fourteen**. Four years later, her husband became **King Louis XVI**.

Unfortunately, many people in France were unhappy with the way the country was run. The rich lived in **luxury**, and Louis and Marie Antoinette were the richest of them all. But ordinary French people were **struggling** to survive, and there were riots over the **high price** of bread.

Still, the king and queen kept buying themselves **magnificent** clothes and **wonderful things** for their houses ... including paintings.

Élisabeth was **terribly nervous** when she first went to the palace – she was nobody compared with the king and queen.

The French court was very formal, and the royal family were very **powerful**. It was hard for Élisabeth to see Marie Antoinette as an ordinary person, like her.

But she and the queen liked each other at once. Soon they became **good friends**, chatting and singing songs together. Once, Élisabeth dropped her paintbox, spilling out her brushes on to the floor, and Marie Antoinette helped her pick them up.

Is she allowed to do that? It's not very... queenly!

Élisabeth quickly became Marie Antoinette's **favourite artist**. She painted portraits of almost all the royal family, but she was best known for her images of the queen – she painted Marie Antoinette more than **thirty** times.

C'est BON!

In **1780**, Élisabeth gave birth to her daughter Julie,
who she adored and would frequently draw and paint.
Two years later, the family went on a trip to Flanders
(northern Belgium) and the Netherlands. There,
Élisabeth saw a very popular work by the famous
artist **Peter Paul Rubens**. It showed his sister-in-law
wearing a straw hat, and Élisabeth was inspired to do
a self-portrait in a similar style, as she'd never seen
anything like it before.

Self-PORTRAIT in a STRAW HAT

In lots of portraits, women are shown looking away as if they are modest or shy. I'm looking right at you!

SMILING

NATURAL HAIR

RELAXED

HOLDING PALETTE AND BRUSHES

In **1783**, Élisabeth asked to join the Académie Royale. At first, the director tried to turn her down, arguing that her application was disallowed because her husband was an art dealer. Then Marie Antoinette intervened for her friend, and the king himself ordered that Élisabeth should be allowed to enter the academy. She was in!

After that, she was able to show her works at the academy's exhibitions called **salons**, which were held every other year. In her first salon, she exhibited *Peace Bringing Back Abundance*, a **history painting** showing two women as symbols of *Peace* and *Abundance*. At the time, these history paintings were considered more important than portraits, landscapes or scenes from daily life. Artists needed special training to create successful history paintings, including **life drawing** experience (drawing nude models), which women weren't supposed to do. But that never stopped Élisabeth before!

I can paint like this too!

At her salon, Élisabeth also displayed a number of portraits, including her *Self-Portrait in a Straw Hat*, which showed her as an elegant society lady and a confident artist. She also showed a portrait of Marie Antoinette that caused a **HUGE SCANDAL** ...

FANCY HEADDRESS

FANCY HAIRSTYLE

In 1778, I painted Archduchess Marie Antoinette, Queen of France, my first official portrait of her.

Très bon.

Looking QUEENLY

FANCY DRESS

This is what a queen is supposed to look like—RICH, important and stately.

The picture of *Marie Antoinette in a Chemise Dress* was a very informal portrait. Many people were **horrified**. They thought it was silly for a queen to be seen in a simple, country-style costume. Queens were supposed to appear grand and royal, wearing the finest silks and beautiful jewels. Marie Antoinette wasn't dressed as she was expected to.

The painting was **shocking** in the same way that Élisabeth was shocking. When she exhibited her work in the way men did, she was asserting herself, showing that she had a right to be in the salons. People thought this wasn't modest or 'feminine'.

And there was another stumbling block. The portrait showed Marie Antoinette as an '**ordinary**' woman. But in a country where so many people were poor and hungry, while the royal family ate huge meals from golden plates, this didn't go down well.

If the queen is just a NORMAL woman like us, WHY do we pay SO much tax for her to live in LUXURY?

The painting was quickly removed and replaced with a different one, showing the queen in much more formal dress.

Despite this, Élisabeth's reputation didn't suffer and her success continued. Élisabeth and Jean-Baptiste held **lavish parties** with delicious food, amazing musicians and wonderful decorations. The parties were famous because they were so expensive! However, Élisabeth herself lived very simply, partly because her husband was still taking most of the money she made.

In **1787**, Élisabeth caused another scandal when she exhibited her *Self-Portrait with Her Daughter, Julie*. This was shocking because she was **smiling**, showing her teeth. At the time, few portraits ever displayed people with open mouths. It was considered impolite, and usually suggested they had something wrong with them!

MON DIEU!

Bonjour!

What's the PROBLEM?

Élisabeth had already shown herself smiling in *Self-Portrait in a Straw Hat,* but in this painting, she was posing with her little girl Julie. It was a 'mother and child' image that reminded people of the Virgin Mary and Baby Jesus. This made it **extra outrageous**! It broke all the rules of how artists should show faces. Critics and artists were **furious**.

However, a lot of people loved it. The picture was fresh, natural and fun. Other wealthy women asked Élisabeth to paint them smiling with their children, and she produced many portraits where the families looked like **typical families**, not like grand people. Élisabeth also painted Marie Antoinette with her children, but the queen didn't show her teeth. Élisabeth was seen as Marie Antionette's official painter, and she did very well by it – until May **1789**, when trouble broke out …

VIVE LA RÉ

France's economy had been doing badly
for years. Ordinary people paid very high
taxes and had to do forced labour. Meanwhile,
the rich lived in luxury!

The commoners had finally had enough. It was
time to rebel!

In June 1789, a party of commoners created
a National Assembly (similar to a parliament),
so that they could make laws without the king.

On 14 July, a crowd stormed the Bastille, a fortress
in Paris where political prisoners were kept,
and the revolutionaries took it over.
The **French Revolution** had begun!

VOLUTION!

In October, a mob of market women who were angry about rising food prices marched to the Palace of Versailles in Northern France. This forced the entire royal family back to Paris. It was the beginning of the end for Louis XVI and Marie Antoinette.

MEW!

The power struggle continued over the next few years. The royal family and many wealthy people were stripped of their titles and riches.

ARGH!

In 1793, both Louis XVI and Marie Antoinette were accused of high treason and had their heads cut off by the guillotine.

Down with the MONARCHY!

It was a **bad time** for the nobility and the royal family, and, as Marie Antoinette's painter and friend, Élisabeth wasn't safe. On the day of the **Women's March on Versailles**, she took her daughter Julie and **fled** to Italy, disguised as a poor woman. Her husband stayed in Paris.

RUN!

FRANCE

ITALY

Élisabeth didn't come home for over **twelve** years. France was a dangerous place. Many of her rich friends were **guillotined**, and her name was on a list of 'counter-revolutionaries' who should be executed for opposing the Revolution.

Élisabeth Le Brun off with her HEAD!

Despite having to flee her home, Élisabeth actually had a **marvellous** time abroad, away from her husband's demands for money and from the disapproving French art world!

Praised for her talent, she was invited to join three national academies. She visited aristocrats' homes and royal courts in Italy, Austria, Russia and Germany. She painted lots of portraits – including one of herself painting Marie Antoinette, to show her **support** for her queen.

In 1802, Élisabeth returned home to Paris, and to her husband. To welcome her back, the staircase was lined with flowers, the bedroom was **beautifully decorated** and there was a crown of gold stars over the bed. Élisabeth thought it was very pretty, but pointed out that he'd paid for it all with her money!

After Élisabeth's adventures abroad, Paris seemed a very dull place. There was no royal court and many of her old friends had sadly not survived the Revolution. She needed a change.

Sigh...

Élisabeth decided to move to England, where she lived for three years and painted many **famous people**, including the Prince of Wales. She also visited Switzerland twice before finally settling back in France to spend the rest of her life painting. In **1842**, aged **eighty-six**, she passed away in her Paris home.

From her humble beginnings, and despite having had no formal training, Élisabeth became a leading portrait painter. She proved that a woman could be a **successful artist**, and that she wasn't afraid to break rules. Élisabeth had great sensitivity towards the people she painted, and she tried to show them in a **natural** and **spontaneous** way that was new and exciting – even if that did sometimes cause **outrage**!

"Before beginning a portrait, engage your model in conversation. Try several different poses and, finally, select not only the most comfortable and natural pose, but the one that suits his or her age and character."

She painted her FEELINGS...

Frida Kahlo

Magdalena Carmen Frieda Kahlo y Calderón, better known as **Frida Kahlo**, was born in **1907**, on the outskirts of Mexico City, Mexico. Her father was a German photographer who had met and married her mother when he moved to Mexico. Frida was a clever, cheerful and playful little girl, and she was her father's favourite of his four daughters. Frida's fun came to an end when at age six she was diagnosed with **polio**, a disease that can cause permanent damage to the muscles. She had to stay in bed for nine months, but her father took great care of her.

Even once Frida was well enough to return to school, her right leg remained weak. She walked with a limp and was cruelly **taunted** for it.

To help her through her loneliness, her father gave her books to read, taught her about nature and showed her how he made photographs in the darkroom. Frida's favourite school subject was biology, and she **dreamed** of becoming a doctor one day.

When she was **eighteen**, tragedy **struck** again. Her school bus was hit by a tram. It was a terrible accident and Frida was very badly injured. After a month in hospital, she was sent home to recover with bed rest and had to wear a plaster body cast – for two long years! To help pass the time and distract from the pain, Frida's parents encouraged her to paint. They made her a special **easel** that she could use lying in bed. They also put a mirror on the ceiling so that she could see herself and make **self-portraits**.

Painting helped Frida find a way through her recovery. And for the rest of her life, she would use art to help her **cope with suffering**.

Mexican communist party youth group

Once she was well enough to leave the house, Frida joined the youth group of the **Mexican Communist Party**. **Communism** is a set of beliefs that say people should own the things that create wealth, such as land and factories. It also says that wealth should be shared evenly between all people, instead of there being a few very rich people and lots of poor people. Frida believed in those **ideals**.

"I'm more and more convinced it's only through communism that we can become human."

Among the Mexican Communist Party members was an artist called **Diego Rivera**, who was famous for painting big wall **murals**. Frida showed him one of her paintings, and asked if he thought she was good enough to become an artist. It was a very brave thing to do! Diego loved her work. He thought it was original, and encouraged her to keep painting.

The two of them **fell in love** and they married in **1929**, even though Frida's mother disapproved. Diego was **twenty-one** years older than Frida, and a successful artist. He was also a very large man and he towered over his petite and pretty wife.

But Frida adored him and was determined to **follow her heart** – plus she never liked being told what to do. It was the start of many changes in her life.

"You are like the ELEPHANT and the dove."

Frida's mother

Frida had discovered art by learning about European **old masters**, and borrowed their style to paint her early portraits. But Diego was passionate about painting Mexican subjects. Under his influence, Frida became more interested in Mexican art and culture.

She changed the spelling of her name from the German 'Frieda' to 'Frida', and began to wear traditional **Tehuana** dress (a style of Mexican clothing embroidered in bold patterns and colours) in most paintings of herself. She also painted in the style of Mexican folk art, using bright colours and simply drawn subjects with no **perspective**.

In 1931, Frida painted one of her first important works, *Frieda and Diego Rivera*. Wearing Tehuana clothes, she appears tiny next to the big, powerful Diego. He is the artist with a palette and brushes, while she is his devoted wife. For many years, Diego was the popular one. But eventually, people started to think that Frida was the better painter.

32

Diego had several **commissions** to paint murals in the USA, so he and Frida went to live there for three years.

They tried to start a family, but soon learned that Frida's body had been too badly damaged in the tram accident for her to have children. Frida was **incredibly sad** and painted some very upsetting images. Many people don't like to talk about such sensitive and heartbreaking events, let alone create pictures about them. But Frida needed to paint so she could **express her feelings**.

I painted a lot of self-portraits –many of my paintings are of me! I used them to think about my feelings towards events or crises in my life. I painted my mixed German-Mexican ancestry, my pain that I couldn't be a mother and myself as an artist, a woman and a wife. **These were the things that made up who I was.**

Itzcuintli Dog with Me, 1938

Everyone has hair on their faces, but people usually expect women to pluck their eyebrows and remove the hair from their top lip. Most painters didn't show women's facial hair, but I made my moustache even more obvious in pictures than it was in real life!

"I am my own muse, the subject I know best"

I didn't believe in changing myself to fit in with other people's ideas of what was BEAUTIFUL.

I laughed a lot, but I look very serious in all my portraits. I wanted to find more unusual ways to show my feelings ...

WOOF!

I painted dogs! The Aztec people, who lived in Mexico, believed that dogs were guides, so I painted dogs when I was trying to make big decisions.

Self-Portrait with Monkey, 1938

I also had lots of pet monkeys, and I painted them too. In this portrait, my favourite monkey, **Fulang-Chang**, is giving me a hug. This shows how important family was to me.

35

In **1933**, Frida and Diego returned to Mexico. Frida hardly painted anything over the next couple of years because her health was very bad. She'd never fully recovered from the tram accident and was in constant **pain**. To help her walk and stay upright, Frida wore braces and surgical corsets, which she sometimes painted. Over her lifetime, she had more than **thirty** operations to try and fix some of the damage to her spine.

Her marriage was difficult too. There were some very **good** things about it ...

They **loved** each other a lot. They were **very proud** of one another's art. Diego once cried with pride when **Pablo Picasso** admired a painting of Frida's!

I admired Frida's ARTWORK and once gave her earrings shaped like hands.

I LOVED them and wore them A LOT.

But there were some **bad** things too …

Diego had lots of girlfriends, which made Frida very **unhappy**.

Frida had boyfriends and girlfriends too, which made Diego **very angry**.

They **often fought**, and sometimes they wouldn't speak to each other.

Their home was actually two separate houses, joined by a bridge. It was as if they didn't know if they wanted to be **together** or **apart**.

Frida and Diego's home became a meeting place for many famous artists and politicians. The **Surrealist** artist **André Breton** visited often, and became a champion of Frida's work.

ANDRÉ BRETON

MARCEL DUCHAMP

Surrealism means '**above realism**'. It's based on the idea that we can find truth and meaning in dreams. Surreal works often put **strange objects** together in odd ways.

RENÉ MAGRITTE

SALVADOR DALÍ

André Breton called Frida a Surrealist, but she didn't think she was. When Frida used **strange images**, they always had a meaning. In her **1946** painting, **The Wounded Deer**, she is showing herself as a lonely, hunted animal in terrible pain. She was using the deer (which was modelled on her own pet deer) to show how she felt – she had just had surgery on her damaged back, hoping it would **free her from pain**, but it failed.

In **1938**, André Breton helped organise Frida's first solo exhibition in New York, USA, which was a **huge success**. The next year, she exhibited her work in Paris, France. The famous Louvre Museum bought one of her paintings, a self-portrait called **The Frame (1939)**, making her the first twentieth-century Mexican artist to be included in their collection.

THE FRAME

In the late **1930s**, Frida's life was often unhappy, but she painted many of her best works during this time. In **1939**, Frida and Diego finally decided they couldn't stay married any longer. **They divorced**, and Frida moved to the house where she was born, La Casa Azul – **The Blue House**.

Frida painted her ***Self-Portrait with Cropped Hair*** right after she divorced Diego. She usually wore feminine dresses in her portraits, but here she's dressed like a man and she has cut off her long hair, which Diego had loved. The only feminine decoration she kept were her earrings. The picture shows how **sad** and **angry** she was, but it also expressed Frida's desire to be independent and to not rely on men.

"There have been TWO great accidents in my life. One was the tram and the other was DIEGO. He was by far the WORST."

But Frida and Diego **missed each other so much** that the next year they got married again! This time their marriage was better, partly because Frida's health was now even worse so Diego **looked after her**, and they didn't argue so much.

After the pair were reunited, Diego went to live with Frida at **The Blue House**.

Later on, Diego built a **studio** for Frida using local materials, and decorated it with Mexican folk art. He lined the ceilings with mosaics and the walls with seashells, and put clay pitchers in the exterior walls to provide nesting spaces for doves and pigeons.

42

The Blue House was also home to Frida's many **exotic pets**, which included **Mexican hairless dogs**, **spider monkeys**, **parrots** and **deer**! They were her constant companions, offering her affection in place of the children she was never able to have.

Meanwhile, Frida's reputation as an artist was growing in the USA and in Mexico. In **1942**, she joined a group of artists commissioned by the government to spread knowledge of **Mexican**

culture. In **1943**, she was featured in several very important exhibitions, such as Peggy Guggenheim's '**Exhibition by 31 Women**' in New York.

But by **1950**, Frida's health was getting **worse** and **worse**. She had problems walking, and eventually had to have part of her leg amputated. She also had several spine operations, and spent lots of time in

hospital. Frida painted powerful images about her **disability** – like *Self-Portrait with the Portrait of Doctor Farill*, which shows her in a wheelchair in front of a picture of her surgeon.

In **1953**, she held her first **solo exhibition** in Mexico. It had taken many years for people at home to see what an important painter she was. By this time, Frida was very ill indeed, and had to travel to the exhibition's opening in an **ambulance**. A truck brought her **four-poster bed**, which was put in the centre of the gallery so that Frida could welcome her guests in comfort and style!

Frida died in The Blue House a year later. Her last painting, **Viva la Vida, Watermelons** was finished just a week before she died. The title means 'long live life'. Its simple scene of **colourful watermelons** is a celebration of life. In Mexico, watermelons are linked with death. On the **Día de los Muertos (Day of the Dead)** there are often images of the dead holding or eating watermelons.

Diego turned The Blue House into a museum of Frida's life and work. Her reputation as a painter has never stopped growing and she is now one of the **best known artists** of the twentieth century. Many books and films have been made about her life, and her bold masterpieces hang in the world's biggest museums.

Frida's work was **deeply personal**, showing her life, her loves, her joys and her sorrows. At the time, most Mexican art took the form of large political paintings, such as Diego's murals, but Frida insisted that **women's personal lives were important too**. Many artists have been inspired by her **honesty**, **imagination** and **determination**.

Paint who you are... BE TRUE to how you really feel.

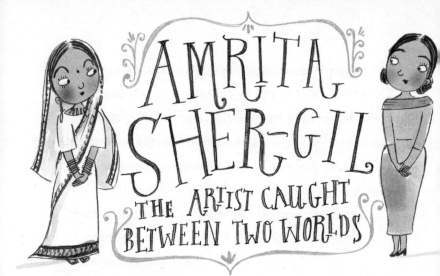

AMRITA SHER-GIL
THE ARTIST CAUGHT BETWEEN TWO WORLDS

Throughout her life, **Amrita Sher-Gil** felt torn between the two sides of her family. Her mother, Marie Antoinette Gottesmann, was a Hungarian opera singer, and her father, Umrao Sher-Gil, was a **Sikh** aristocrat and scholar.

THE SHER-GIL FAMILY

The couple had met in India in **1912**. Marie was visiting the country as a companion to the Sikh princess Bamba Sutherland, and was instantly impressed by Umrao.

He studied **Sanskrit** (an ancient Indian language) and astronomy, and was also a very good amateur photographer. They got married and moved to Budapest, Hungary, where Amrita was born in **1913**. Her sister Indira arrived just over a year later.

Amrita's early childhood was spent in **Budapest**. The Sher-Gils were well connected – they knew aristocrats, artists and intellectuals, as well as politicians and diplomats – so they often went to **glamorous** dinners and parties. However, there weren't many Sikhs in Hungary then, so **the family stood out**.

In **1921**, when Amrita was **eight**, her parents moved back to India. At that time, India was still part of the **British Empire**, though a lot of Indians wanted their country to be independent. Umrao's family owned a house and land in **Simla** (now called Shimla), a town in the Punjab at the foothills of the Himalayas.

Simla was the summer residence of members of the **British Raj**. Many British people lived there, working for the civil service, the army or for businesses. Some very wealthy Indian families lived in Simla too, and many of them felt they had much more in common with the British, who lived a life of luxury and privilege, than with poorer Indian people.

Simla was the perfect place to escape the thick Indian **heat** that filled India's southern cities. In the cooler temperatures, people could ride, play croquet, watch racing cars and have lots of **extravagant** parties!

Although they lived in India, most British people there still wore their own style of clothing and often behaved as if they were still in Britain. In some of the photographs Umrao took of his daughters, they are wearing **British-style dresses**. In others, they are draped in **Indian saris**.

Amrita enjoyed going to parties with her family, but what she really **loved** to do was draw and paint. When she was **eight**, her parents arranged for her to have proper painting lessons, but they didn't go very well …

Amrita's teacher told her that what she painted should look as much like real life as possible, and so he made her draw the same thing over and over again. This made Amrita **very cross**! Why should something have to look real to be considered art? Furious, Amrita told her parents that the lessons were a waste of time, and they quickly found her a new teacher!

"I DETESTED the process of colouring in the drawings of picture books and I NEVER allowed grown-ups to draw things for me to colour in … I always drew and painted everything myself."

Despite this, Amrita's love for art **grew** and **grew**.

When Amrita was **eleven**, her mother took her to live in Florence, Italy, for a few months. She went to a Catholic school, but was **expelled** for drawing a nude figure! It was on this visit that Amrita first became interested in the works of the Italian masters and other European painters, who would influence her early paintings.

They returned to Simla later that year. Amrita grew close to her uncle Ervin from Hungary, who visited the family. He was a painter and he encouraged Amrita to **draw from life**, getting the family's servants to pose as models.

It was around this time that Amrita began to notice how women's lives were often **controlled** by others. In her diary, she wrote about a wedding she attended between a **thirteen-year-old girl** with a **fifty-year-old man**. It upset Amrita that the girl had been forced into the marriage in order to please her parents.

DIARY

OLD

It's not right

When Amrita was **sixteen**, she and her family moved to Paris, France, where she trained as a painter for five years. This was very **unusual** because most Indian women weren't encouraged to study or work outside of the home. Amrita was lucky that her parents were **artistic**, **liberal** and **wealthy**. They allowed her to **follow her dreams**.

Amrita revelled in the **excitement** of city life, enjoying nights out with her new artistic friends. They didn't follow **old-fashioned** rules about how women should behave. Amrita had lots of boyfriends and girlfriends, and she didn't worry about what other people thought of her. She was a **rebellious**, **determined** person who always wanted to do things her own way. Paris suited her perfectly.

PARIS
FRANCE

my friends

Paris!

at work

She impressed her teachers and the other students with her talent, strong opinions and passion for painting. Amrita was interested in drawing human figures, so she made many sketches of male and female nudes to improve her technique. She also began to paint with **oils**, producing **still lifes** and many portraits of friends, and she painted herself over and over again, in different moods and outfits.

Like Frida Kahlo, Amrita used self-portraits as a way of **trying to understand herself**.

Amrita felt that her **identity** was made up of many different parts, and those parts didn't always fit together. There was her life in India, and her life in Europe. Her family expected her to be **sophisticated** and **well dressed**, but behind closed doors she was **artistic** and **messy**. She could be confident and outgoing, but she sometimes hid herself away too.

In **1932**, aged **nineteen**, Amrita painted a picture called *Young Girls* that captured these feelings. It shows her sister Indira wearing fashionable European clothes, and her French friend Denise, who is only half dressed. Indira looks elegant and at ease, while Denise is more awkward, with her face hidden beneath her untidy hair.

People were very **impressed** by this painting. In **1933**, it won a gold medal from the **Grand Salon**, and Amrita was made an associate member. She was the **only Asian** and the **youngest** person **ever** to have that honour.

I'm calling it YOUNG GIRLS.

Although her work was well known and admired in Paris, Amrita wanted to go back to India. She felt that the country's **unique colours, light and natural environment** would be wonderful things to paint, and would help her develop her own style.

But her father wasn't so keen on the idea. He was worried that she might **embarrass** the family because of her rebellious ways. He wrote to her asking her to stay in Europe.

Amrita loved her father and was hurt by his letter, but she also **didn't like being told what to do**. She went back to India in **1934**.

NOBODY tells me what to do!

57

When Amrita returned to Simla, she was invited to lots of glamorous parties with generals and maharajahs (Indian princes). But Amrita **wasn't interested** in that world. She **wanted to show** what life was like for Indians **who were poor**, as she felt sad that they were often ignored. So, she travelled across the country to meet Indian villagers.

She spent time talking to young women about the pressure they were under to behave in certain ways – above all, **having to marry men** that were chosen by their parents. In **1935**, she painted *Three Girls*. It depicts three young village women sitting and waiting for something, and though they are dressed in brightly coloured saris, their faces are **sad** and they are surrounded by **shadows**. The picture hints that their future lives may not be happy.

In the **1930s**, the art scene in India wasn't thriving in the same way that it was in Paris. India has a wonderful history of art, but art schools were under British rule at the time and **didn't teach** students anything about Indian painting or sculpture. They only spoke about great **European painters of the past**.

India was ready for change. There was still a strong mood of **nationalism** (loyalty to your country) as Indians began to seek independence from Britain. Amrita supported this, even though her family had close ties to the British Raj.

Amrita decided it was time for her to learn more about India's **rich history of art**, which nobody had ever taught her. She visited museums and studied collections of early miniature paintings. And in late **1937**, she toured the south of the country, where she was **dazzled** by the bright colours and by the people who lived there. She visited important Indian art sites, such as the ancient **murals** of the **Ajanta caves**, which she found beautiful and inspiring.

FASCINATING!

The Ajanta Caves

So detailed!

a guide to
indian miniature painting

From the 1500s to the early 1900s, many **magnificent** paintings were made for the royal courts of India. These small-scale, highly detailed pictures were made as illustrations for books, or as individual paintings. There was a huge variety of styles, including **Mughal** and **Pahari**.

Mughal painting is the art of the **Mughal Empire**, which ruled most of India from the 1500s to the 1800s. Influenced by **Persian** art, the paintings were subtly coloured and lifelike, mainly showing elegant scenes from court life and history.

Pahari painting comes from the Himalayan hill kingdoms of North India, and flourished in the 1700s and 1800s. These paintings used bright colours and bold patterns to show scenes from **Hindu** myths and legends.

. **huge influence** on her art,

, to southern India. She saw for

or many people were, particularly those

illages in the countryside. They did hard

m... al labour and were exhausted, yet they kept on going. Amrita was moved by their experiences, and felt guilty that nobody in the cities where she'd come from knew of their struggle. **She vowed to represent their lives in her work.**

She developed a style that blended techniques of modern European art with Indian themes. Her paintings showed **ordinary life**, using **bold shapes** and **strong colours**. This was very unusual at a time when Indian art mostly featured landscapes and characters from ancient literature or mythology, painted in pale colours.

"I am personally trying to be an INTERPRETER of the LIFE of the people, particularly the life of the POOR and SAD."

Amrita was proud of her new style and what she was doing – she finally felt like she had **found her artistic identity**.

SOUTHERN VILLAGERS GOING to MARKET

When Amrita was **twenty-five**, she moved to Hungary to **marry** her cousin, Victor Egan, who was a doctor. Many people were surprised because Amrita definitely didn't seem to want to settle down. But Victor was a good friend whom she could rely on, and she wanted to be more **independent from her parents** – marriage would help her to do that.

Amrita and Victor left Hungary before the **Second World War** began in **1939**. They moved to an Indian village called **Saraya**, where Amrita continued painting. Her style now headed in a **new direction**. She was more concerned with the moods and meanings she could create with colour and shape, so she made the figures in her art **simpler**, while making the **colours richer**.

Her work started to make an **impression** on the Indian art world. Most critics loved it, and some even called her the **greatest painter of the century so far**. However, she wasn't yet popular with the people who actually bought art – they preferred more traditional styles. Several rich aristocrats refused to buy her work at auction.

Although Saraya was a very poor village, Victor and Amrita lived comfortably there on her rich uncle's estate. But Amrita didn't like it. It was too quiet and there weren't many other creative types to spend time with, so she soon **grew bored**.

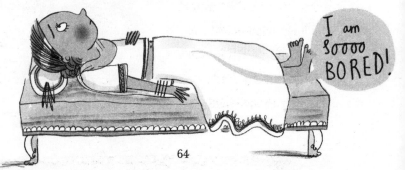

In **1941**, Amrita and Victor moved to **Lahore**, one of India's main cultural centres at the time. Lots of writers and artists lived there. It was **lively, interesting** and there were people who **cared** about Amrita's art and ideas. She wanted Indian painters to break away from outdated art traditions and **find their own style**.

"Produce something VITAL, connected with the SOIL, something essentially INDIAN."

Amrita quickly became very well known and respected. She was set to have her first major solo exhibition in December **1941** – a **huge achievement** for a young woman – when, very suddenly, she **sadly** died. She was only **twenty-eight**.

Indian News

SHOCK DEATH OF ARTIST AMRITA SHER-GIL

AMRITA SHER-GIL SOLO EXHIBITION

In her brief but **brilliant career**, Amrita had a huge influence on Indian art because she showed just how **rich** and **wonderful** traditional Indian styles were, and how they could be **modern** too. She is a role model for women artists all over the world as an **independent artist** who created her own pioneering style, and put ordinary people, **especially women**, at the centre of her work.

Through her art, Amrita daringly bridged the **gap between** Europe and India, and between rich and poor. While her work barely sold in her lifetime, today she is known as one of India's most celebrated artists, and is recognised as a **National Treasure**.

Käthe Kollwitz

Her ARTWORK inspired HOPE

Born in 1867 in East Prussia (now part of Russia), KÄTHE KOLLWITZ was the fifth of seven children. Käthe was nervous and shy, so her family nicknamed her 'KÄTHUSHCEN' (meaning 'Little Käthe').

Although they had a big family, Käthe's mother and father made sure all their children had the best possible education. Her father soon saw Käthe's ARTISTIC POTENTIAL – she would spend hours cutting out paper dolls and painting them with WATERCOLOURS. He loved the things she made. Even though Käthe was still very young, he was keen for her to become a painter, so he arranged for her to have lessons in different artistic skills.

When she was SEVENTEEN, Käthe got engaged to a medical student called Karl Kollwitz, which her father wasn't at all happy about! He worried that marriage would make Käthe forget about her art, so the next year he sent her to Germany to study drawing ...

Karl

BERLIN
SCHOOL FOR
WOMEN ARTISTS

I love ART.

He hoped she would think again about the engagement once she'd had a taste of ARTISTIC LIFE.

Käthe didn't change her mind and kept seeing Karl, who was also studying in Berlin. So, in 1888, her father sent her away again, this time to the Women's Academy in Munich. There, Käthe began to study PRINTMAKING, and she was BRILLIANT at it – much better than she was at painting.

PRINTMAKING is where an artist creates an image on one surface, such as metal or wood, known as a plate. Then they apply ink over the plate and carefully print the image on to another surface (usually paper). There are different kinds of printmaking techniques, including ETCHING, LITHOGRAPHY and WOODCUT – which Käthe was an EXPERT at all of them.'

Paper

Ink

Printing Plate

While she was away, Käthe THOUGHT HARD about getting married. Would it stop her from being an artist? Karl supported her ambitions, and now had a job as a doctor in Berlin, which would give them enough money to live on. Käthe LOVED Karl, and she was tired of her father telling her what to do.

Wedding Day

Käthe and Karl were married in 1891, and had two sons – first Hans, in 1892, then Peter four years later. Käthe continued her artistic career once she became a mother, as giving it up would have made her unhappy. She was able to do this because she could afford to pay a housekeeper. But for many women, it wouldn't have been an option. Käthe knew how LUCKY she was.

I'll look out for you.

A few years later, when one of her art-school friends couldn't continue to work as well as look after her child, Käthe and Karl helped her by ADOPTING her son.

The Kollwitz family lived in a POOR part of Berlin. Käthe saw how difficult life was for many people there, especially women. They were often the ones responsible for looking after parents, husbands and children, which was tiring work, physically and emotionally. Käthe would sit and talk to the women who attended Karl's clinic, LEARNING about their lives and LISTENING to their stories.

Käthe wanted others to know these WOMEN'S STORIES too, and to recognise their struggles. So she depicted it in her art, hoping it would make people sad and angry, and INSPIRE them to make a better, fairer world.

71

A WEAVERS' REVOLT
1893~97

Käthe's first important work was a **series** of six LITHOGRAPHS based on the true story of a weavers' uprising in 1844 ...

The weavers worked hard, but were paid very little and had TERRIBLE living conditions.

My child is sick.

I llness and death are all around.

Ink

They marched to DEMAND CHANGES were made, and even attacked their employers' homes.

Several of them were killed by the army, ending the revolt.

Käthe had seen a famous play about this event in 1893, and it reminded her of the downtrodden life that many poor people were experiencing at that time. She wanted to use the weavers' story to show their SUFFERING, but also their TREMENDOUS BRAVERY.

Käthe produced images of all the different parts of the story, showing the run-down places where the workers lived, their DETERMINATION on the march and the SAD way the rebellion ended. The series was a huge success, and Käthe was awarded a GOLD MEDAL for it in 1899.

In 1898, Käthe began teaching at the BERLIN ACADEMY FOR WOMEN ARTISTS. But she found it difficult to combine teaching with her own work and her family life, so after five years, she left.

At the time, she was working hard on her etchings, including another important series, *PEASANTS' WAR* (1902–08). This was about the 1524–25 German Peasants' Revolt, in which hundreds of thousands of peasants fought against the greedy, mean nobles who ruled over them. The nobles were able to buy more weapons and experienced soldiers, and so the peasants were defeated. When Käthe retold the story in her prints, she showed WOMEN as VICTIMS of the nobles' cruelty, as LEADERS of the rebellion and finally as MOTHERS mourning the dead.

In 1907, Käthe won a very important German art award, the VILLA ROMANA PRIZE. This allowed her to spend a year living and working as an artist in Florence, Italy. She took her son Peter with her to help him recover from a disease called tuberculosis. She didn't find the city very inspiring, but enjoyed spending time in the beautiful countryside with Peter.

Around 1910, Käthe started making sculptures in stone and clay. Käthe enjoyed EXPLORING new art forms, and as her sons got older she looked forward to having more time for her work.

Then the FIRST WORLD WAR broke out and everything changed ...

GERMANY DECLARES WAR

1 AUGUST 1914

On 28 July, one month after the assassination of Austrian Archduke Franz Ferdinand by a Serbian nationalist, Germany's ally Austria declared war on Serbia. In response, on 30 July, Serbia's supporter Russia began readying its army to fight Austria.

Despite Germany's demands for Russia to halt its troops, the country resisted. With this, Germany have **declared war** on Russia.

Germany now urgently needs fine young men to join the army.

Sign up today

Like many young men, Käthe's **TWO SONS** volunteered to join the army. Käthe was upset because she believed that countries should **COOPERATE** with one another, and felt it was stupid that they should go to war.

Peter and Hans

Most people expected the war to last just a few months, but it went on for four years, finally ending in **1918**. More than nine million soldiers and approximately ten million civilians were killed. It was one of the biggest wars in history.

Tragically, Peter died in battle in **OCTOBER 1914**, just two months after the war began. Käthe was **DEVASTATED**. She despised the war, but worried that if she spoke out against it, she would betray what Peter had died for. She wrote in her diary:

"Is it a break of faith with you, Peter, that I can now only see MADNESS in the WAR"

77

Käthe became a **pacifist**, meaning she believed war and violence are wrong and shouldn't be used to settle disputes. Towards the end of the war, when the German government called for more men to join the army, she made a public statement begging them to stop.

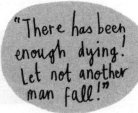

"There has been enough dying! Let not another man fall!"

Käthe decided to create a MEMORIAL SCULPTURE for Peter and all the young men who had gone to war. She worked hard but wasn't happy with the design. After five years of trying, she put the project aside.

Käthe was the MOST IMPORTANT German female artist of her time. In 1917, she was offered a large exhibition at the Paul Cassirer Gallery in Berlin to mark her FIFTIETH birthday. And in 1919, she became the first woman to be elected a member of the PRUSSIAN ACADEMY OF ARTS, which meant she was given her own studio.

The war had left Germany in a very BAD SITUATION. Germany was blamed for all the loss and damage that other countries had suffered, and was made to give up land and pay huge amounts of money to make up for it. This was hard on ordinary German people who had suffered and lost family too. To some of them it seemed unfair that they were being punished with further poverty, when they had already suffered enough. Due to this, some German politicians called for another war to improve Germany's fortunes, and unfortunately, MANY PEOPLE listened.

Käthe couldn't believe anyone would want another war. She tried to remind people of the HORRORS they had seen in the last one. She started work on a series of woodcuts showing the suffering of common people, and made several anti-war posters. Many of the images show MOTHERS and CHILDREN looking terrified or helpless.

In April 1931, she at last finished her MEMORIAL to Peter – two SCULPTURES called *THE GRIEVING PARENTS*. They went on display at the NATIONAL GALLERY IN BERLIN before being moved to Belgium in 1932, where they were placed near to her son's grave in the VLADSLO GERMAN WAR CEMETERY.

THE GRIEVING PARENTS

The two granite sculptures show Karl and Käthe grieving for their son. Karl is holding himself upright, wrapping his arms round himself. Käthe is hunched over in pain. Although simple, the sculptures are POWERFUL images of grief and loss.

Käthe's memorial wasn't just for Peter but for ALL the young men who died, and all the parents who mourned them. Around TWO MILLION Germans lost their lives in the war. Käthe wanted to show her own sadness in a way that would reach out to others and help them express their feelings too. She also wanted to remind the world of the MISERY that war causes, so they wouldn't make the same mistake again.

But not enough people paid attention.

In 1933, the **Nazi Party** came to power in Germany. It was led by Adolf Hitler, a politician who promised to make Germany great again. He blamed the country's problems on foreigners, political rivals and groups of people he hated, such as Jews. Nazi laws were CRUEL and RACIST. Käthe had spoken out against the Nazi Party in the 1933 election. So when the Nazis took over as leaders of the country, they forced her to resign from the PRUSSIAN ACADEMY OF ARTS.

PRUSSIAN ACADEMY OF ARTS

82

The Nazis CONTROLLED all forms of communication in Germany, including art, books, films and music. Anything that went against their beliefs was changed, removed or destroyed. Käthe was a working mother who hated war, so her work was REMOVED from museums and galleries.

In 1936, Käthe and Karl were visited by the GESTAPO (the Nazi secret police), who threatened to put them in a **concentration camp** unless Käthe agreed to support the Nazi Party and give the names of other anti-Nazi artists. They also expected women to stay at home and look after the family. She refused. Luckily, the Gestapo didn't carry out their threat, though no one really knows why. Käthe and Karl were the lucky ones. They might have escaped, but millions of other people would die in Nazi concentration camps before the evil was ended.

In September 1939, Adolf Hitler invaded Poland, which led Britain and France to declare war on Germany. It was the start of the SECOND WORLD WAR. Karl died the following year after a long illness, aged SEVENTY-SEVEN. And Käthe's grandson Peter was killed fighting in the war in 1942. During the bombing of Berlin in 1943, Käthe's home was BOMBED by British planes and many of her artworks, photographs and letters were destroyed. Käthe was filled with DESPAIR.

She died of heart failure on 22 APRIL 1945, two weeks before the end of the SECOND WORLD WAR.

Käthe's story is TRAGIC, but it's only one of millions of SORROWFUL stories from the war. It was this that Käthe wanted to show in her art – that people everywhere were suffering. Käthe hoped her POWERFUL images would highlight to those in charge what was really going on. Käthe had a difficult life, but she stayed COURAGEOUS and never gave up on what she believed in.

Her commitment to her art proved that women could be HIGHLY SUCCESSFUL artists as well as have families. The women in Käthe's work are shown as strong and brave, as well as loving. They fought for what they believed was RIGHT. Käthe's story shows how art can help people cope with challenging times, and INSPIRE US to make the world a more positive place.

DAME LAURA KNIGHT

she found INSPIRATION in all walks of LIFE...

Lace

DAME LAURA KNIGHT was born into a family of lace-makers in Derbyshire, UK, in **1877**. She was the youngest of three daughters. Laura's mother Charlotte brought the girls up on her own, while teaching art to make enough money to get by. She even found time to give all her daughters art lessons. Laura soon showed a natural gift for it, and always preferred pencils and paper to toys.

When Laura was **TWELVE**, she went to live with her great-aunt's family in France. They were able to pay for her schooling, and Laura hoped she might eventually go to **ART SCHOOL** in Paris.

Paris

Unfortunately, she had a tough time in France. Although Laura had learned some French at school in England, she struggled to make herself understood and found it difficult to make many friends. Tragically, her sister Nellie also passed away while she was there. Laura felt **LONELY** and **HOMESICK**.

But there were happy days too. For one thing, Laura was able to practise her art. Her uncle gave her a new paint box, which she treasured for many years. And she spent time at an artist's studio, painting still life and copying his pictures.

Her aunt and uncle also took her to markets and fairs, as well as circuses, which Laura found thrilling. The **CIRCUS** would always hold a special place in her heart.

Then came more bad news. In **1890**, the family lace-making business failed. There was no more money for Laura's education, or for art school. She had to go home to England.

WOW!

Luckily, Laura's mother managed to get her a free place to study at the **NOTTINGHAM SCHOOL OF ART**. She was only **THIRTEEN**, which made her the school's youngest ever pupil, but Laura tried hard to fit in and was talented enough to show she belonged there.

However, female students were offered fewer opportunities than male students, who were given life-drawing classes. At the time, it was considered improper for women to see **NAKED** people, let alone paint them. This made Laura **CROSS** – she didn't think it was fair that she should miss out on important training, just because she was a woman.

LIFE-DRAWING CLASSES

Draw from life! Nude models help you:
LEARN about the human body
PRACTISE your portrait skills
UNDERSTAND how to draw people

Everyone* welcome!

(*Women not included. Life drawing is INDECENT for women! Female students can draw plaster casts of statues instead.)

HOW RIDICULOUS!

Laura was given a hard time by her teachers too. She was told off for '**DRAWING LIKE A MAN**' because she was too heavy-handed with her pencil, and advised to develop a more '**FEMININE**' style.

On the upside, Laura made friends with a very talented student called **HAROLD KNIGHT**. He always talked to her properly about art instead of treating her differently.

But life soon took another **UNEXPECTED TURN** for Laura ... Shortly after starting at the school, her mother was diagnosed with cancer. So Laura, aged just **FOURTEEN**, had to take on some of her mother's teaching duties. She put her hair up and pretended to be **TWENTY**! Laura was nervous about teaching, especially as some of the students were older than she was, but she **TRIED HER BEST**.

Laura's mother died in **1893**, leaving Laura and her sister Eva (whom she called 'Sis') heartbroken, and with almost nothing to live on.

The next year, Laura won the Prince of Wales scholarship to the South Kensington School of Art. She was paid **£20** a year for two years, which was a big help to Laura and Sis.

Laura left the **NOTTINGHAM SCHOOL OF ART** in **1895**. Then in **1898**, she and her sister moved to live in **STAITHES**, a fishing village on the Yorkshire coast. There she found a little cottage, where she had her own **STUDIO SPACE**.

Laura fitted in well with the local people and with the artists' community there. She painted **FISHERMEN** and other villagers as well as views of the sea. In summer, she spent time on the **BEACH**, by the **ROCKS** and wherever children were playing, making notes and drawings. In the winter, the studio got very **COLD**, so she burned lots of her unsuccessful drawings and paintings to keep it warm!

Harold and Laura had remained close throughout their studies and, in **1903**, they got **MARRIED**. Art was always a very important part of their lives, and on their honeymoon they visited the National Gallery in London **EVERY DAY**. Over the next three years, they spent long periods living in an **ARTISTS' COLONY** in Holland, studying Dutch masterpieces and working on their painting skills.

ADMITS TWO NATIONAL GALLERY

HOLLAND NETHERLANDS

TICKET FOR TWO HOLLAND

In **1907**, Laura and Harold moved to Cornwall to become part of a group of artists called the **Newlyn School**. It was a lively group and Laura quickly settled in. They spent many hours painting together on the beach. Laura would paint children playing on the sand, and she also hired models from London who were happy to **POSE NAKED**, sometimes outdoors. Some local people got **RATHER UPSET** about that, but Laura was finally making up for all those lessons she'd missed at art school.

Laura found her own style, which was influenced by the bright colours and beautiful backgrounds of French **Impressionist** works. Her painting **BLOSSOMED** – and so did her career, as her work became known nationally and internationally.

JULY 1908

I spent another beautiful day on the beach at **NEWLYN**. I love the warmth of Cornwall, the wonderful light in the afternoons and the carefree way children play on the sand. My sketches for my paintings are coming along well too.

What fun!

ONE OF HER BEACH PAINTINGS WAS EXHIBITED AT THE ROYAL ACADEMY IN 1909 AND WAS A HUGE SUCCESS!

Now it's finished, I think I'll call it 'On the Beach.'

1911

I have never painted so fast as I have today! I asked the **DANCER** Dolly Snell to pose for me, wearing one of my home-made evening dresses, Harold's old jacket and a hat with a green feather. **SHE LOOKED LIKE A DUCHESS!**

In the morning it was overcast and cloudy, but then it suddenly changed to bright sunshine. I didn't want to stop painting, so I just repainted the background! I finished my painting in just one day! It shows all the things I love about life in **NEWLYN** - the light, the landscape and our **FREEDOM** to be as **ECCENTRIC** as we like, even if people think we are **ODD**.

I'll name it 'the GREEN FEATHER'.

THE NATIONAL GALLERY OF CANADA BOUGHT *THE GREEN FEATHER* FOR £400! A HUGE AMOUNT OF MONEY AT THE TIME.

Do you like my hat?

Toodle pip!

Laura was suddenly a **SUCCESS** and was even invited to Buckingham Palace to meet the Prince of Wales! At last she didn't have to worry about money. Still, Laura knew what it was like not to have money, so she was **ALWAYS CAREFUL** to save where she could.

When I went to BUCKINGHAM PALACE, I insisted on taking the bus home.

LONDON BUS

GOOD CUP OF tea

DREAM

9

In **1913**, Laura caused a commotion when she displayed her new piece, ***SELF-PORTRAIT (WITH NUDE)***, where she pictured herself painting a nude model. Laura was still bitter about having not been allowed to paint naked bodies at art school, so this was her **PROTEST**.

As well as showing a nude female figure, Laura's painting depicted Laura herself in a pose and dress that were **UNCONVENTIONAL** for the time. She had her back to the viewer, and instead of wearing her best Sunday dress, she was in casual clothes and showing herself at work! Critics were **STUNNED**.

The Royal Academy refused to show the work, and some newspapers wrote horrible things about her for painting it. But Laura didn't care. She wanted to portray herself as an independent professional, and declare that women artists were entitled to paint in the same way as men. Today, the painting is in the **NATIONAL PORTRAIT GALLERY**, and many people think it's her masterpiece.

But within a year, the newspapers had something much bigger to write about. The **FIRST WORLD WAR** was declared in **JULY 1914**. Men from all over the country joined the British Army. In **1916**, Harold received his call-up papers, which meant he had to join the army. But Harold believed **VIOLENCE WAS WRONG**, so he refused. This was a very unpopular opinion. People who would not fight were often called cowards and traitors, and could be sent to prison. Harold was sent to do back-breaking hard labour on a farm instead.

Laura understood Harold's principles and **RESPECTED** them, but she was commissioned to work as a war artist herself. She found a place to live near the farm where he worked so that she could see him, and kept painting, although it wasn't easy. She loved to paint on the beach, but in wartime there were laws that **BANNED** people from drawing and sketching on coastlines, in case they were German spies. Laura used to **SNEAK AROUND**, hiding in bushes by the sea, so she could make sketches for her paintings.

When the war ended in **1918**, Harold was allowed to leave the farm work. Harold and Laura moved to London in **1919**, but they returned to Cornwall for the summers throughout the **1920s**. In the city, Laura found inspiration at the **THEATRES** – especially a glamorous Russian dance company called **BALLETS RUSSES**. But instead of painting their performance, she wanted to capture the dancers in more **RELAXED** moments.

The **1920s** was a busy decade for Laura. In **1926**, she visited America with Harold, who had been commissioned to paint surgeons at Johns Hopkins Hospital in Baltimore. Like many hospitals in the USA at that time, there was racial **segregation**, which meant that Black and white patients were in different wards. Laura painted staff and patients from the Black community, including **PEARL JOHNSON**, who campaigned against segregation.

Laura sketched us getting read[y]

PEARL JOHNSON

Laura and I became good friends. I introduced Laura to CIVIL RIGHTS.

Dame Laura Knight

WOW!

Back in London, Laura's **STAR CONTINUED TO RISE**. She was made an associate member of the **ROYAL ACADEMY** in **1927** – only the second woman to receive such recognition in the twentieth century. This was **HUGELY EXCITING** news and she was delighted. Two years later, she would be honoured as a **DAME OF THE BRITISH EMPIRE** (which is the same as a man getting a knighthood). Laura was the **FIRST** female artist ever to be given the title.

Around this time, Laura also got to know the performers of the **BERTRAM MILLS CIRCUS**. The circus was a very exciting show, with performers from all over the world wearing **SPECTACULAR** costumes to do their nail-biting, hilarious and mind-boggling acts. As with the ballet dancers, Laura liked painting the performers behind-the-scenes, **TALKING** and **RELAXING** in their stage outfits.

The CLOWNS

In **1929**, Laura got a letter from a man called Major Evelyn Atherley. He loved the **CIRCUS** as much as Laura did, and wanted her to paint a portrait of his dog **BLINKERS** with the famous clown **WHIMSICAL WALKER**. Laura agreed, and the Major was thrilled! So much so that he kept asking Laura to add more and more circus characters ...

Can we add another clown? AND an elephant?

I'll try my BEST.

Lots of critics sneered at the painting, called *CHARIVARI*, which means *THE GRAND PARADE*. But Laura didn't care, and the Major **LOVED** it.

woof!

In **1929**, Laura joined the **BERTRAM MILLS CIRCUS** on their national tour, and spent four months living with the **CLOWNS** and **ACROBATS**. Laura developed a real understanding of the life of the travelling performer, and she loved it.

"I was as much a part of the CIRCUS as anyone in the show, used to putting up with anything."

Laura was extremely curious about other people, and liked to paint **UNUSUAL** or **OVERLOOKED** subjects. In the **1930s**, she began to paint the world of **HORSE RACING**. She was a regular visitor at the Epsom Downs racecourses, where she set up a mini studio in the back of an old, rented Rolls Royce and painted the crowds of spectators.

Laura's work was well known and respected by this point. In **1936**, she wrote a bestselling book about her adventures, called *OIL PAINT AND GREASE PAINT*. She was also elected President of the **SOCIETY OF WOMEN ARTISTS**, (an organisation that celebrates and promotes art created by women) and was the first woman to be made a **FULL MEMBER** of the **ROYAL ACADEMY**. (She and Harold were the Royal Academy's first married couple!)

Everything seemed to be going well for her ... but war was coming back to Europe.

When the **SECOND WORLD WAR** began in **1939**, Laura was asked to do a recruitment poster for the **Women's Land Army**, an organisation that employed women in farming jobs while the men went to fight.

Laura became an official **WAR ARTIST** again, painting women in the armed forces, including women who were operating huge balloons that defended cities against enemy planes. She also painted women doing factory jobs. A lot of Laura's art was meant to **ENCOURAGE** more women to join up for war work. It was difficult to keep the balloons and factories running with so many of the male workers away at war. It was dirty, smelly, noisy hard work ...

BUT IT NEEDED DOING!

In **1943**, Laura met **TWENTY-ONE**-year-old **RUBY LOFTUS**, who worked at a factory where weapons were made. It was dangerous work – if not done exactly right, the guns might **EXPLODE** when they were fired! Most factory workers would have had at least eight years of training before they were allowed near such machines. Ruby only had a couple of years to train and yet she could do the work **PERFECTLY**.

Laura decided to paint Ruby, and made her look like a **CONFIDENT** and **SKILLED** heroine because that's what she was – working to keep Britain running while the war went on in Europe. The painting was a great success and was made into posters. Ruby and Laura were both interviewed a lot and became quite **FAMOUS**!

BE MORE RUBY LOFTUS

LET'S WIN THIS WAR!

The war ended in **1945**, but Laura still had one more big war painting to do. In **1946**, the surviving leaders of Nazi Germany were put on trial in **Nuremberg**, Germany, for the **TERRIBLE CRIMES** carried out under their leadership. Laura was now nearly **SEVENTY**, but she was made a war correspondent and given a place in the broadcasting box with the reporters, so she could make sketches of all the prisoners.

Laura was **HORRIFIED** by what she heard at the trials. She painted the men and their lawyers in a very realistic way, but depicted the courtroom without walls. Instead, she set the witness box in the bombed-out, **BURNING RUINS** of Nuremberg. Her picture doesn't let anyone forget what these men did. The critics didn't like the painting, but now many people think it's one of the **GREATEST WAR PAINTINGS OF ALL TIME**.

After the war, Laura went back to the subjects she **LOVED**. She worked backstage in **LONDON THEATRES**, painting actors, but spent most of her time painting landscapes from her country home in Worcestershire.

In **1965**, the **ROYAL ACADEMY** held an exhibition to **SHOWCASE** Laura's life's works, which was the first time a woman had been given this **HONOUR**. Five years later, in July **1970**, Laura died peacefully at home.

Laura painted many **DIFFERENT WORLDS**, from the **BALLETS** and **THEATRES**, to **PERFORMERS** and **TRAVELLERS OF THE CIRCUS**, to **WARTIME BRITAIN**. Daring, broad-minded and committed to her work, Laura challenged people's expectations of what women can do, paving the way for other women artists who followed in her footsteps.

"Even before I could speak or walk, I drew. There was no question of my purpose in life."

EMILY KAME KNGWARREYE

THE ARTIST WHO NEVER STOPPED DREAMING

Emily Kame Kngwarreye was an **Aboriginal** Australian born sometime around **1910**. She grew up in a very remote desert area called Alhalkere, in the country's **Northern Territory**. There the land is rocky and the earth is red and bare, with only a few plants and trees. For some people the desert might seem like a tough place to live, but it is **sacred** to the Aboriginal community.

My home.

Aboriginal Australians have lived in Australia for more than **50,000** years, and they have their own **art** and **culture**. White Europeans started **colonising** the country in **1788**, taking over land and settling there to live. Many Aboriginal Australians were killed and many more were driven out of their lands.

'Aboriginal Australian' is the name used for all the **Indigenous** peoples (those who lived on the land first, before the colonisers came). There are lots of different groups, speaking more than **200** distinct languages. Today, they make up just over three per cent of Australia's population.

In the **1940s**, white European cattle farmers began taking over the land of Emily's people, and they called it **Utopia** ('The Good Place'). It didn't belong to them – it belonged to the **Alyawarre** and **Anmatyerre peoples.** But the cattle farmers had guns. They overpowered the Aboriginal people, making them move to small areas and treated them almost like slaves.

Emily had to work as a **servant** to white families, doing jobs such as cleaning and cooking. When she grew up, she worked at a cattle station, looking after the cows. She also worked with camels, helping carry supplies to a mine. She wasn't properly paid for her work, but was given goods including sugar, flour, tea and old clothes in return.

UTOPIA

TEA

Although Emily's people had lost their land, they still had a strong sense of their culture. Emily never went to school, but she was educated in the sacred tribal traditions of her **Anmatyerre people** and eventually became an elder (a leader who knows the tribe's culture and history). She learned to create **sand paintings** and paint **decorative patterns** on women's bodies as part of an ancient ceremony called **awelye**. She was also a guardian of the women's sacred sites in her clan country of Alhalkere.

ART AID

Art is at the **heart** of many **Aboriginal rituals,** and is usually created with natural materials from the land. Some ceremonies include sand paintings, which are designs drawn on the desert floor.

They can be small ...

... or as BIG as a football pitch.

The artists make colours from **ochre,** a kind of clay that comes in many colours such as red, yellow, brown and white. The paintings aren't made to last – after the ceremony, the wind will blow them away.

CEREMONY

Aboriginal women perform **awelye** to show respect for their country, for example by telling stories of their ancient past, or by declaring responsibility for their community. The ceremonies reflect the women's role as **nurturers**, taking care of the people and land, healing, feeding and looking after everything.

We paint animal and plant designs on to each other's bodies.

There is singing, chanting and DANCING.

Australian Aboriginal culture is the **oldest** living culture in the world, and **awelye** art may be the oldest living art form.

Most of Emily's life was spent living and working in and around Utopia. She had very little contact with the outside world. But in **1976**, a law was passed that said Aboriginal people could claim rights to their traditional **homelands**. At last, there was a chance for Emily's community to get their stolen land back! Soon after that, the government introduced a women's adult **education** programme, offering courses to women who had little or no education. Emily belonged to a Utopia women's group, and, in **1977,** they attended a workshop to learn the art of **batik**.

Batik is a way of decorating cloth using dye and wax. Designs are often made up of **lines** and **dots**, just like the sand painting and body painting in Aboriginal culture. Emily made abstract patterns on silk, using lines and dots, as well as plant and animal figures. People quickly saw that she was **incredibly talented**. Here's how you can have a go at doing it yourself ...

Before you start:

Batik making is a very creative thing to do and great fun. But it can be a bit of a tricky process, so **ask an adult** to give you a hand!

116

Batik: A Step-by-Step Guide

YOU WILL NEED:

Scissors

Clothes iron

Saucepan (to melt the wax)

Lightweight cotton cloth

Newspaper

Pencil and paper

Beeswax (or batik wax)

Large knitting needle

Fabric dye

Paintbrush

1. Cut out a piece of cloth (20 x 30 cm is a good size to start).

2. Place the cloth on a table or work area, then draw a simple design on to it.

3. **With the help of an adult,** put the wax in the saucepan and gently heat it until it melts.

4. Using the knitting needle, trace over your design with the wax.

5. With a paintbrush, cover your cloth in dye.

6. Next, cover the entire cloth with a second layer of wax.

7. Once the wax has cooled and hardened, place the cloth between two sheets of newspaper, then iron over it. Repeat until all the wax has been removed.

8. Your artwork is finished!

In **1979**, there was a trial to decide who had the right to the Utopia land. Emily and other women from her community performed an awelye ceremony before government officials, using their art and culture to show their **connection to the land**. And they won! The land belonged to the Anmatyerre and Alyawarr peoples again.

Around ten years later, when Emily was nearly **eighty**, the Utopia Women's Batik Group held an exhibition of their work. Lots of people came to see it. Afterwards, the group began a new project – painting on canvas, using **acrylic** paint. Using acrylics gave Emily even more **freedom** to **express herself**.

Emily's first painting was called *Emu Woman*. The coloured dots and lines were based on painted body markings used in awelye ceremonies. They often resemble plant and animal images from **Emily's Dreaming** (see next page), while the curves and loops mimic the way the paint might look on a woman's body.

Emu Woman was a huge success. People from the art world were **amazed** by Emily's **powerful**, **confident** painting and were keen to see more of her work.

GASP!

WOW!

So talented!

THE DREA

Aboriginal religion and culture are between **40,000** and **65,000** years old. They are based on the **Dreaming,** which is the word used to describe the story of how the **universe came to exist, how human beings were created** and **how the Creator meant people to live.** Australian Aboriginal people believe that the world was shaped by **Spirits** who came from below the Earth and above the sky. They made **everything** ...

The word 'Dreaming' can't really be translated into English and it's very hard for those not part of it to properly understand.

trees

rivers

hills

waterholes

animals

plants

The Spirits gave people their **land,** their **special important** objects and their **Dreaming.**

In the DREAMING people are part of NATURE.

MING

Different Aboriginal people have **different beliefs**. Some believe in Ancestors who were animal Spirits. Emily's *Emu Woman* painting shows **respect** to the Emu Ancestor.

The places where the Spirits did important things, or were turned into parts of the landscape, are **sacred**. The Aboriginal people who live in sacred places, like Alhalkere, are the **guardians** of the Dreaming. Their responsibility is to **pass on** the stories through ceremony, ritual, song and dance, and to preserve and protect the land with its sacred sites. **Making art is part of the Dreaming too.**

my DREAMING was my beliefs about creation and the nature of the WORLD, the stories of my ancestors and my relationship with the land.

121

Working on canvas in acrylic paint **opened up** Emily's art. It was much easier and faster to do than batik, and she could mix bright, bold colours to get the effects she wanted.

Once she had discovered acrylics, Emily worked with **incredible speed**, often completing a painting in a day. Some people say she worked so hard and so fast because she was very old when she started painting. She knew so much about the world and her culture, and didn't have a lot of time left to **express** all the things she had to say.

Emily first drew widespread attention when her paintings were displayed in Sydney in **1989**. After that, her career soared and she travelled all over Australia. She held **five** one-woman shows in **1990**, as well as group exhibitions. In **1992**, she was awarded an **Australian Artists Creative Fellowship**. It was the first time an Aboriginal person had won this very important award. By the next year, her work had been shown in more than **fifty exhibitions** all over the world – just five years after she picked up a paintbrush for the first time!

Emily had become an **international star** almost overnight. Lots of galleries wanted her work, and she was often pestered by art dealers who tried to buy her paintings cheaply.

But despite her newly found fame, Emily lived **traditionally**, the way she always had, and **shared** her earnings with her family and community. In order to make money and help her people, she kept on painting even though she had crippling arthritis (pain in the joints) and her eyesight was failing.

AUSTRALIA NEWS

AMAZING ARTIST

ART WORLD NEWS

EMILY IS A STAR

Like nature itself, Emily's painting style was always changing as she boldly experimented with **new styles** and techniques.

At first, she used detailed **dots** and **lines** based on the colours and shapes of body markings used in awelye ceremonies – like emu tracks, plants and seeds, painted in red, yellow, black and white.

Then, she switched to using larger brushes, working **faster, more loosely** and on a **larger scale**.

During the early **1990s**, she started creating huge landscapes, using brighter pastel colours in blues and pinks. These canvases were covered in clouds of dots and lines that gave an **impression** of desert colours in summer, or the night sky.

Later, she took a
new direction,
criss-crossing
the canvas with
bold, simple lines in
strong, dark colours.

People who watched Emily paint
said it was like watching the **movement
of a dancer**. She would change the brush from
her right hand to her left, and even use a brush in both
hands at once, dipping the brush in paint and dragging
it across the canvas like a **dancer's feet** drawing
patterns in the sand.

One of Emily's most famous works is her *Big Yam Dreaming*, a huge black-and-white painting. It took Emily just two days to paint. She didn't make any test sketches or plans, but just sat on the canvas to paint and worked her way out to the edges, **without changing anything.**

The painting is **inspired** by the paths that yam roots take underground, causing the Earth's surface to crack. Yam roots were very **important** in Emily's Dreaming, as her people followed the cracks to **find food** in the desert. Often, the first things she painted on a canvas were yam tracking lines. And her middle name, 'Kame', means the seeds and flowers of the yam plant.

Emily's art always came from her **connection** to her people, land and culture. Alhalkere was the source of all her inspiration. Even her nose piercing was a **tribute** to her ancestor Alhalkere, a huge arched rock.

Emily mostly spoke **Aboriginal languages**, and knew very little English. When she was asked to explain her paintings, her answer was always the same:

"... whole lot, that's whole lot, AWELYE, ARLATYEYE ARKERRTHE, NTANGE, TINGU, ANKERRE, INTEKWE, ATNWEREI KAME. That's what I paint."

Awelye is the women's ceremony with body painting.

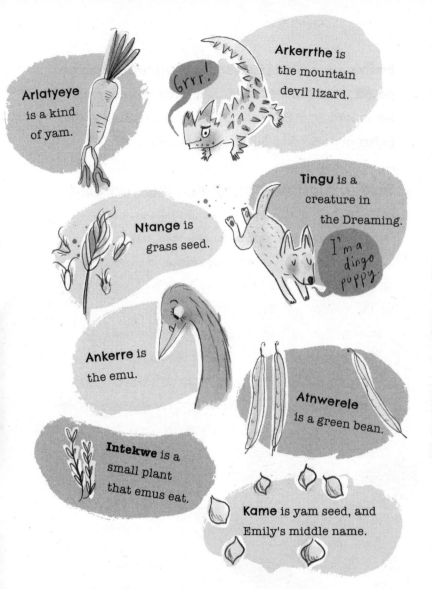

Arlatyeye is a kind of yam.

Arkerrthe is the mountain devil lizard.

Grrr!

Tingu is a creature in the Dreaming.

I'm a dingo puppy.

Ntange is grass seed.

Ankerre is the emu.

Atnwerele is a green bean.

Intekwe is a small plant that emus eat.

Kame is yam seed, and Emily's middle name.

Emily was explaining that whatever she painted was **part of her Dreaming,** and **the whole of her life**.

Emily died in **1996**. Her painting career had only lasted **eight** years. She had never had formal art training, had hardly travelled and didn't know anything about Western or modern art – except for the small Utopia group she worked with. All her **inspiration** came from her **culture, her home** and her **Dreaming**.

Emily's rise as an artist came at a time when the Australian descendants of **colonists** were starting to admit how **badly** Aboriginal people had been treated, and were trying to **change** things. Without that development, Emily might never have created art that people all over the world could see. How many other people might have been **great artists** if only they had had the chance? **How many people like Emily never got to hold a pen or paintbrush?**

FAITH RINGGOLD

SHE STITCHED TOGETHER UNTOLD STORIES...

Faith Ringgold was born in Harlem, New York, in **1930**. Her family were African American, and Harlem had recently become an **incredibly exciting** centre of Black American culture. People called this time the ...

HARLEM RENAISSANCE!

THE GREAT MIGRATION AND THE HARLEM RENAISSANCE

For many years, Black people were forced to work as slaves in the USA, especially in the South. Slaves were freed after the **American Civil War** (1861–65). But many Southern States passed laws that discriminated against Black Americans. There were racial segregation laws that meant Black and white people were kept separate, and many Black Americans were violently attacked and even killed. Millions of Black Americans moved North, where the prejudice wasn't so bad. This was called the Great Migration.

Many of these migrants ended up in Harlem, which became the centre of an amazing explosion of culture in the 1920s.

African Americans worked together to create wonderful art and ideas. They became writers, musicians and dancers ...

WRITERS LIKE ...

ZORA NEALE HURSTON

LANGSTON HUGHES

MUSICIANS LIKE ...

FATS WALLER

LOUIS ARMSTRONG

Renaissance means 'rebirth'. Once they were free from the cruel laws of the South, the people of the **Harlem Renaissance** were able to spread their wings and use their talents.

DANCERS LIKE ...

JOSEPHINE BAKER

WOW!

By the mid-**1930s**, the Harlem Renaissance was coming to an end. Meanwhile, the country was facing economic crisis – lots of banks and companies closed, people lost their jobs and many people went hungry. This period of history was called the **Great Depression**.

Although Faith's family didn't have much money, she still had a **wonderful childhood**. Her father, an ex-minister, was a gifted storyteller, and her mother was a fashion designer. They took good care of her, and she grew up surrounded by artists, musicians and writers.

But Faith's childhood wasn't all fun. She suffered from bad **asthma** so had to spend lots of time in bed, where she drew and coloured pictures, and she learned to sew.

Her parents were very keen for her to get a university degree. Faith loved art, but at that time, art was still considered a **job for men**. So, she started off taking a degree in art and education, followed by a **master's degree** in art, at the **City College of New York**. Frustratingly for Faith, the college only taught art that had always been popular in the Western world, such as Greek sculptures and paintings by old masters. If she wanted to learn about other types of art, she would have to **seek it out herself**.

While she was studying, Faith got married and had two children, but unfortunately her marriage didn't work out and she and her husband separated four years later.

Faith worked as a teacher for a while, and went on a long trip to Europe with her mother and daughters, visiting many **wonderful museums**. She painted too. But although people liked her work, she found it hard to sell. Most of the art traders and gallery owners in New York were white people, which made it very **difficult** for a Black artist – especially a Black woman artist – to find places to show their work.

Then, in **1962**, Faith married Burdette Ringgold, who everyone called Birdie. He helped her take her work around to art galleries, hoping that they would show her paintings ...

In 1963, Faith met New York City gallery owner Ruth White. Faith showed Ruth some of her work – still life paintings of flowers and landscapes done in a traditional European style.

Ruth looked at the paintings for a long time, then
finally told her:

Ruth didn't explain why, and Faith couldn't stop
thinking about it. As Faith drove back to Harlem with
Birdie, she went over the meeting again and again.
Then she realised something ...

Faith never found out if that was what Ruth had
meant or not. But it didn't matter – she had found
her **inspiration**!

In the **1960s**, America was in the middle of a violent struggle for equal rights for Black people, known as the **Civil Rights Movement**. There were marches, fights and terrible riots. During this time, Faith started painting her *American People* series, which was about race relations in the USA. Many of the pictures, such as *The In Crowd* painted in 1964, show white people ignoring Black people, shutting them out or threatening them.

Shh.h.!

The In Crowd

Her last painting in the series shows Black and white adults in business suits and smart clothes **fighting**. In the middle of the painting, two scared children, a white boy and a Black girl, hold on to each other. The painting shows that **racism** and violence are things people learn to do. Children aren't born hating other people, and adults should **take care** of children instead of making the world a bad and scary place.

Help!

ARGH!

Finally, Faith found a gallery that would show her work, and they planned to hold a solo exhibition of her *American People* series once it was finished. The problem was, the pictures were **HUGE** and Faith didn't have much space to paint at home, especially with two small children running around.

She moved into the gallery to use it as a studio, leaving Birdie at home. Faith's mother took her children to Europe for the summer. She was able to work on her art because her whole family helped and **supported** her.

THE AMERICAN DREAM

Well done, mum.

clap clap

Faith believed more Black people and women should have the chance to show their art. When an important New York art museum held an exhibition on modern artists and didn't include any Black people or any women, Faith and many other artists **protested**. She also helped start a group for Black women artists called the ...

WOMEN STUDENTS AND ARTISTS FOR BLACK ART LIBERATION

all art is important!

BLACK ART in GALLERIES

WE NEED 50% WOMEN ARTISTS

In the early **1970s**, Faith created an
enormous mural in a women's prison.
Before she started work, Faith interviewed
some of the inmates and asked them what
they would like to see in a piece of art. They
said they wanted to see gender equality.
They wanted to see women in roles that
have traditionally been saved for men.

Faith's painting, called **For the Women's House**,
illustrates for the first time women in different
situations that were **rare** or **unimaginable** for the
time. She included things such as woman police officers
directing traffic, female professional basketball players, a
female doctor and a female president.

By this point, Faith was eager to discover more styles from Africa and Asia. On a trip to Amsterdam in **1972**, Faith saw **thangka** – Tibetan paintings that were done on cloth or silk and framed with beautiful fabric. Faith wanted to try this for herself so she started work on a series of cloth paintings that **imagined** what African women's experiences under slavery were like.

Next, Faith set to work making costume masks out of fabric, beads and raffia inspired by traditional African tribal costume. Named the *Witch Mask Series*, the masks were worn in Faith's first performance piece.

THE WITCH MASK SERIES

As well as masks, Faith made life-sized soft sculptures made of cloth, with foam bodies and coconut-shell heads. In the late **1970s**, Faith visited **Nigeria** and **Ghana** to see the art there, especially the masks, for herself. Faith had a wonderful time – she loved how many different styles there were, and that each had a different story to tell. She was keen to bring the styles she had seen into her own work, so she started using traditional Nigerian and Ghanaian textiles.

Faith was **changing the face** of the New York art world because ...

SOFT SCULPTURES

She used AFRICAN styles and TRADITIONS instead of Western ones.

She put BLACK women at the centre of her art!

She used art forms often seen as women's crafts, like sewing and work in fabric. These were treated as less important than painting or sculpture.

Faith found inspiration in lots of different places. But all her ideas came together when she started to make **quilts**.

African American quilting is a very **old tradition**. Enslaved Black women were often made to do work such as quilting, sewing, spinning and weaving for rich, white households. After the American Civil War, many African Americans were freed but they were still very poor. So women made quilts out of torn scraps of cloth, old clothes and sacks. The quilts were a way for these women to make art, and would often display beautiful patterns and colours. One of the most famous quilt artists was a freed slave named **Harriet Powers**. Her elaborate quilts depicted Bible stories and natural events such as forest fires and falling stars.

Harriet Powers

Faith's grandmother had taught her how to quilt when she was a little girl. In **1980**, Faith made her first quilt artwork, called *Echoes of Harlem*. She painted portraits of her Harlem neighbours on cloth, showing all the **different communities** who lived side by side. Then, her mother helped piece them all together into a quilt. This would be their last collaboration before Faith's mother sadly passed away.

Faith started to make painted '**story quilts**' with modern subjects, using a combination of images and handwritten text. People loved them and they sold very well.

Faith's quilt ***Tar Beach*** is a story set in **1930s** Harlem. It's about a little girl called Cassie Louise Lightfoot and her family. In the story, Cassie looks up at the stars and dreams she can fly. The quilt shows her flying over the city one summer night.

The message of the quilt is happy and encouraging. Three years later, Faith turned it into a **children's book** that used bright colours and wonderful pictures to tell a magical story about African American life, culture and families. The book won many awards, and Faith went on to write other children's stories based on her quilts.

What a DREAM!

During her career, Faith has won many awards, and her art is displayed in major galleries and museums.

She **fought** for the right of Black women to have their art seen and valued, paving the way for many other Black female artists. Her **hard work**, **daring** and **determination** helped show the Western art world that there was important art out there from different countries and cultures, and that women had lots to say. Later in her life, she still worked as an artist, writer, activist and teacher, with exhibtions all over the world. She never stopped **weaving together** wonderful stories in her work.

When Faith was told she couldn't do something, she found a different way to make her voice heard – and the voice of others too, proving that **everyone's experience is important**. Those who wonder if their story is worth telling or if their picture is worth painting should think about Faith – **and just do it**!

PEGGY GUGGENHEIM
THE COLLECTOR WHO PUT MODERN ART ON THE MAP

PEGGY GUGGENHEIM wasn't actually an artist herself, but she was a passionate admirer of art, and created one of the **MOST IMPORTANT** collections of modern European and American art in **HISTORY**.

Peggy was born in August **1898**, and grew up in New York, USA. Her parents were incredibly rich and the family lived like royalty, but Peggy's childhood was unhappy. Her mother Rosa wasn't very interested in her children, and often left Peggy and her sisters alone. Peggy adored her father Benjamin, but he was always travelling and was rarely at home.

Then, in **1912**, when Peggy was **THIRTEEN**, tragedy struck ...

THE TITANIC

Peggy's father Benjamin embarked on the maiden voyage of the *TITANIC,* a huge passenger ship which set sail from Southampton, England, towards New York, in **1912**.

WOW! This is the largest, fastest ship of the age.

TITANIC

It is UNSINKABLE.

But just before midnight on **14 April**, the ship hit a huge iceberg.

ARGH! The ship is going to sink!

People began to panic, desperate to get off the boat. But there weren't nearly enough lifeboats to save all the passengers from the freezing Atlantic waters.

THIS WAY!

Benjamin helped as many women and children as he could into the lifeboats. But there wasn't room for him.

WOMEN and CHILDREN FIRST!

We will go down with the ship, like gentlemen.

Benjamin dressed in his best clothes, placing a rose in his buttonhole. He then waited for the ship to sink, alongside other **BRAVE** men including his valet, **VICTOR GIGLIO**.

Victor and Benjamin

Their bodies were never found. More than 1,500 people died on the *Titanic*.

Peggy was **DEVASTATED** – she couldn't believe she would never see her father again.

Benjamin had also lost a lot of money in his businesses. Peggy's family were still very rich compared to most people, but they were no longer **INCREDIBLY** rich – not like her Guggenheim relatives. The family had to move to a less luxurious apartment, and couldn't have as many servants.

Peggy didn't feel she belonged with the other rich girls at school any more, or with her rich relatives. She decided to **REBEL**, which included shaving off her eyebrows!

ARGH! We only have one maid. What will people say?

HA! How do they like me now?

Peggy wanted to do something **USEFUL** when she left school, but she didn't know what. Women from her world didn't usually take jobs. She thought she could become a secretary, so she tried to learn typing and **SHORTHAND** (a quick form of writing that uses symbols and abbreviations), but she wasn't very good at it and the other girls made her feel like an outsider. Eventually, she gave up.

Meanwhile, on the other side of the world, the **FIRST WORLD WAR** was tearing Europe apart.

In **1917**, the USA joined the fight. While American men went off to war, people at home did what they could to help the soldiers and keep the country running. Peggy **KNITTED HUNDREDS** of socks for soldiers. In fact, it became a bit of an obsession, and she would even take her knitting to the theatre and restaurants!

In **1918**, she got an official job helping the war effort, advising new officers where to buy uniforms and equipment at the best price. During this time, she got engaged to a pilot before he was sent overseas to fight, though she didn't marry him in the end.

The war ended shortly after Peggy turned **TWENTY**, and on her **TWENTY-FIRST** birthday she was given the **FORTUNE** she'd inherited from her father. Now she had enough money to live independently. She decided to **GET AWAY** from her glamorous wealthy family and friends, and make something of her life. She travelled around North America on a **GRAND TOUR** while she thought about what to do.

NORTH AMERICA

WOW!

Where next?

What will I do with my life?

In **1920**, Peggy was in the privileged position of being able to take an unpaid job in a New York bookshop that sold very modern, **EXPERIMENTAL** books. It was owned by two women called **MARY MOWBRAY-CLARKE** and **MADGE JENISON**, who often held exhibitions for new artists. Peggy **LOVED IT**.

She quickly became friends with many of the artists and writers that she she met, such as the writer **F. SCOTT FITZGERALD** and the photographer **ALFRED STIEGLITZ**. She liked talking to them about their work and **LEARNING** about their lives.

The atmosphere is so creative!

Mary

Madge

F. Scott Fitzgerald

156

Alfred Stieglitz

20th CENTURY PAINTERS

MODERN ART

So much to learn n.

Mary and Madge only gave Peggy boring work like filing, and hardly ever let her into the shop to sell books. They also didn't pay her and gave her cheap books instead! But Peggy didn't mind. In fact, she used to sweep the the floor wearing an expensive coat and pearls. She wanted to **SOAK UP** the atmosphere at the shop and tried her best to **BELONG**.

Peggy started buying paintings from her new artist friends, and gave money and food to struggling artists and writers. She learned lots about art, visited galleries and got to know the work of modern painters such as ...

PABLO PICASSO

HENRI MATISSE

PAUL CÉZANNE

MY PASSION for ART began to grow.

Peggy travelled to Europe in **1921**. She wanted to see all the art she possibly could, from ancient Greek and Roman art to the very latest modern paintings. It was her own unique art education!

"I soon knew where every painting in Europe could be found."

She visited many cities in Belgium, the Netherlands, Italy and Spain. But it was Paris, France, that **CAPTURED HER HEART**. It was full of artists and ideas. This was the kind of exciting life that Peggy wanted. She made friends with many of the most important artists and thinkers in France, like **PABLO PICASSO**, **HENRI MATISSE**, **JEAN COCTEAU** and **MARCEL DUCHAMP**.

PABLO PICASSO   HENRI MATISSE   JEAN COCTEAU   MARCEL DUCHAMP

During this time, Peggy got married to an artist with whom she had two children. Unfortunately, the marriage was very unhappy, and they eventually divorced. Peggy married again, this time to a writer, but sadly he died a few years later. She felt lonely and frustrated. Once again, she wasn't sure what to do with her life.

In **1937**, Peggy's mother died, leaving her another fortune. Although Peggy's family frowned on many of the things she did, **ART COLLECTING** was not one of them. It was actually a family hobby, Peggy's uncle Solomon had a priceless collection of old masters.

So, the following year, Peggy decided to use her fortune to open an **ART GALLERY** in London, England, called **GUGGENHEIM JEUNE**, named after herself and a famous Parisian gallery. It showcased modern art, and included the work of artists who hadn't yet been '**DISCOVERED**' by the art world, but many of whom would go on to be some of the most celebrated artists of all time. Her gallery **CHANGED THE WORLD OF MODERN OF ART**.

The gallery was a big success with critics, but Peggy didn't sell enough paintings to make it work as a **BUSINESS**. She also realised she didn't like showing work for a short time. She wanted to have a large, permanent collection of the art she loved, and to share this with others. So, she decided to start a **MODERN ART MUSEUM** in London.

And her collection began to grow ...

161

By September **1939**, war had been declared, and Germany had already invaded Poland. It was a frightening time. But Peggy had a mission.

As the German army prepared to attack Western Europe, Peggy went through the art galleries and studios of Paris, buying work by **PABLO PICASSO, SALVADOR DALÍ, JOAN MIRÓ, PIET MONDRIAN, MAX ERNST** and many more. She bought a lot of pieces cheaply because many artists and art dealers knew that the Germans would invade soon, and needed the money to get away. Peggy kept buying art, even once the Nazis had invaded France and the army was marching towards Paris! This was particularly **RISKY** because Peggy was Jewish, and the Nazis **persecuted** Jewish people.

Ugh! They decided my collection wasn't worth saving.

Paris was invaded in June **1940**. It was time for Peggy to go back to America, where she would be safe. She asked the Louvre Museum in Paris to take care of her collection, but they refused.

This was a big problem. The Nazis **DESTROYED** art they didn't like. If they got hold of Peggy's collection, it could all be burned. But it was difficult to transport a large art collection, especially in wartime. In the end, Peggy packed up the paintings and sculptures in crates along with pots, pans and sheets, and shipped the lot to New York as household goods.

HOUSEHOLD GOODS

Tum te tum...

163

ART of this CENTURY

Peggy finally left France in July **1941**, along with her two children and the artist **MAX ERNST**, whom she married later that year. She had wanted to set up a museum in London, but with Europe at war, she needed to find a **HOME** for her collection in America.

In October **1942**, Peggy opened a new museum and gallery called **ART OF THIS CENTURY**. It was the most exciting contemporary art gallery in New York. She displayed her art collection and held exhibitions of European artists as well as the work of several unknown young Americans, such as **MARK ROTHKO** and **JACKSON POLLOCK**, who went on to become very famous for their work as **abstract expressionists.** She also held a show for female artists called **EXHIBITION BY 31 WOMEN** that included Frida Kahlo.

Peggy's gallery introduced young American artists to the most exciting, modern European painting styles. Always on the lookout for **NEW TALENT**, she would buy paintings by undiscovered artists and sometimes give them money to live on while they painted.

ABSTRACT EXPRESSIONISM

America's first internationally important art movement, known as ABSTRACT EXPRESSIONISM, became a success thanks to Peggy.

The paintings don't try to show people or objects. Instead, the artists use just lines, shapes or colours to show emotions. Two of the painters leading this movement were MARK ROTHKO and JACKSON POLLOCK.

Lots of Mark Rothko's paintings showed large blocks of colour with the edges blurred together. He didn't say if they meant anything – he left it to people to decide what they thought.

Jackson Pollock splashed and dribbled paint on to the canvas to create a mix of colours and textures.

Many critics didn't understand the style and said it wasn't 'PROPER PAINTING'. Peggy's support made a huge difference. Now, they are some of America's LEGENDARY artists.

It's the next BIG thing!

After the war ended in **1945**, Peggy published a book about her life called ***OUT OF THIS CENTURY: CONFESSIONS OF AN ART ADDICT***. It caused a big **SCANDAL** because she talked about all her

boyfriends, who included many well known artists and writers. Her family was so **SHOCKED** that they tried to buy all the copies to stop anyone else from reading it!

In **1946**, Max and Peggy had divorced and Peggy was fed up with New York. She closed her gallery in **1947**, and exhibited her collection at an important art show in Venice, Italy, introducing the work of **POLLOCK** and **ROTHKO** to Europe for the first time. Peggy had always loved Venice, a beautiful city that had been untouched by the war. She'd visited before, but this time she decided to stay.

A year after the exhibition, she bought a **1700s** white stone ***palazzo*** (a splendid house built for very wealthy people) called Venier dei Leoni on the Grand Canal.

Peggy's Palazzo

She turned the gardens, cellar and servants' rooms into galleries to display her collection. Every summer she opened her collection to the general public, and it soon became a tourist attraction.

The rest of the *palazzo* was Peggy's **HOME**. There was art in every room. She had so many paintings she even had to stack them in her bathroom, where they got splattered with toothpaste! Her bed was a huge silver sculptural art piece. The Venetians called her ...

The Last Duchess!

Peggy's bathroom

In the **1970s**, Peggy agreed to leave the *palazzo* and her collection to the Solomon R. Guggenheim Foundation, created in **1937** by her uncle Solomon. But she insisted that the collection had to stay in the *palazzo*, and not be moved to the **SOLOMON R. GUGGENHEIM MUSEUM** in New York – a big modern building that she called 'my uncle's garage'.

Peggy died aged **EIGHTY-ONE** on 23 December **1979**, and her ashes are kept in the garden of her museum. *THE PEGGY GUGGENHEIM COLLECTION* is one of the **FINEST** museums of modern art in the world.

Although Peggy Guggenheim wasn't an artist herself, she was very important. As the other stories in this book tell us, artists need galleries to show their work – and people to buy it, talk about it, and share it. Peggy's support helped art and artists **FLOURISH** – many of the most **INFLUENTIAL** artists of the 20th century might never have been discovered if it wasn't for her. She championed modern art when most people in the art world didn't believe it was worth anything, and she saved many important artworks from the Nazis, who would have burned them. Thanks to Peggy, hundreds of thousands of visitors can see the **WONDERFUL** art she collected every year.

"I dedicated myself to my collection. I made it my life's work... I am not an art collector, I am a museum."

GLOSSARY

Abstract expressionism: an art movement in the 1940s and 1950s, characterized by brush-strokes and mark-making.

Ally: a person, group or country that supports another. In wartime, allies often fight together.

Alyawarre people: a community of indigenous Australian people, or language group, from the Northern Territory.

American Civil War: a war that took place in the United States from 1861 to 1865, between the Union (Northern States) and the Confederacy.

Anmatyerre people: a community of indigineous Australians, or language group, from the Northern Territory.

Apprentice: a young person who studies a craft or skill by learning alongside a master.

Batik: a technique for decorating cloth using wax and dye on fabric.

British Empire: the group of countries and territories across the world once ruled by the United Kingdom.

British Raj: the name used to describe British rule in India between 1858 and 1947.

Civil Rights Movement: a protest movement opposing racial segregation and discrimination against Black Americans in the 1950s and 1960s.

Colonist: a person or group who settles in an area and takes control of it.

Commission: the act of instructing and paying an artist to produce a particular piece of artwork.

Communism: a political and economic system where all major resources are owned by the government and are equally shared among the people.

Concentration camp: a place where the Nazi Party sent prisoners during the Second World War.

French Revolution: a period of unrest in France, from 1789–99, when the people overthrew the royal family and took control of government.

Great Depression: a period of economic crisis in the 1930s that began in the United States and quickly spread across the world.

Harlem Renaissance: a revival movement in African American culture in the 1920s and 1930s.

Impressionism: a 19th-century French art movement based on spontaneous, outdoor painting with visible brush-strokes.

Indigenous: the name for people who lived somewhere first.

Life drawing: artwork made from drawing naked people from a live model.

History painting: a painting depicting people or an event from history.

Maharajah: an Indian, Hindu prince.

Master's degree: an advanced degree given by a university for specialist work.

Mexican Communist Party: a political party in Mexico based on communist beliefs.

Mughal Empire: an empire that ruled a large part of South Asia from the 1500s to the 1800s.

Mural: a large painting usually on a wall or ceiling.

Muse: a person who is the inspiration for an artist's work.

Nationalism: the name for strong attachment and dedication to a particular country or nation.

Nazi Party: a political party in Germany led by Adolf Hitler, prominent from the 1930s to 1940s.

Newlyn School: a group of impressionist artists who lived in Newlyn and St Ives, Cornwall, England, in the 1800s.

Nuremberg (trials): a series of trials charging former leaders of Nazi Germany with war crimes.

Old masters: the term used to describe European artists who worked between the 1300s and 1800s.

Pacifist: someone who believes war and violence to be wrong.

Pahari painting: a style of painting from the Himalayas, usually using bright colours and bold patterns.

Palazzo: an Italian name for a type of house, usually for wealthy people.

Persecuted: treating someone badly because of their race or political or religious beliefs.

Perspective: a way of painting or drawing that makes some objects appear closer than others.

Salon: a French term for a big exhibition showing work from different artists.

Segregation: the separation of people in their daily lives based on race.

Series: a collection of an artist's work linked by either a common theme or style, or made during the same time.

Shorthand: a quick form of writing that uses symbols and abbreviations.

Still life: a style of art that depicts inanimate objects.

Surrealism: an experimental art movement from the 20th century that shows unrealistic and dream-like scenes.

Tehuana: a traditional Mexican style of clothing, usually heavily embroidered.

Thangka: a style of Tibetan paintings on cloth or silk and framed with fabric.

Women's Land Army: a British organisation of women who worked on the land during the First World War and Second World War.

Women's March on Versailles: an important event that took place at the beginning of the French Revolution, in which women marched to Versailles and demanded bread for their families.

FURTHER READING

If you want to find out more about any of the fantastically great women in this book, the books and websites below are brilliant resources.

BOOKS

Sanchez Vegara, Maria Isabel, (2016), *Frida Kahlo (Little People Big Dreams)*. London: Frances Lincoln Children's Books.

Jackson, Sharna, (2021), *The Met Faith Ringgold: Narrating the World in Pattern and Colour - What The Artist Saw*. London: DK.

Pankhurst, Kate. (2016), *Fantastically Great Women Who Changed the World*. London: Bloomsbury.

Pankhurst, Kate. (2018), *Fantastically Great Women Who Made History*. London: Bloomsbury.

Pankhurst, Kate. (2019), *Fantastically Great Women Who Worked Wonders*. London: Bloomsbury.

Pankhurst, Kate. (2021), *Fantastically Great Women Scientists and their Stories*. London: Bloomsbury.

(2018), *V&A Introduces - Frida Kahlo*. London: Puffin.

Ignotofsky, Rachel, (2020), **Women in Art: 50 Fearless Creatives Who Inspired the World**. London: Wren & Rook.

WEBSITES

Tate Kids. https://www.tate.org.uk/kids

Britannica Kids. http://kids.britannica.com/kids/

BBC Bitesize. https://www.bbc.co.uk/bitesize/subjects/zn3rkqt

National Geographic Kids. https://www.natgeokids.com/uk/teacher-category/art/

National Gallery of Art. https://www.nga.gov/audio-video/video/kids.html

Peggy Guggenheim Collection. https://www.guggenheim-venice.it/en/art/in-depth/peggy-guggenheim/about-peggy/

Frida Kahlo Foundation. https://www.frida-kahlo-foundation.org/

Faith Ringgold. https://www.faithringgold.com/art

THANK YOUS!

I've been doodling and scribbling since childhood so to do a whole book about amazing female artists has been a real treat! I have been working on this book as I returned to work after having my daughter. Learning about these incredible artists and what they had to say through their art really fired up the creative part of my brain again after many sleepless nights, pandemic lockdowns and general mum busyness. I hope you feel inspired to pick up a pencil or paintbrush after reading it too!

This is the bit of the book where I get to say a massive thank you to the team of fantastically great people who have helped me put it together! (Authors and illustrators don't make books all on their own, oh no! The best ideas happen when you can bounce thoughts off the brilliant people you work with.)

Firstly, I'd really like say how much I appreciated the support of the Bloomsbury non-fiction team who have now moved on to new adventures in publishing ... Isobel Doster (editor extraordinaire on this book and many of the other Fantastically Great Women books), Saskia Gwinn and Sharon Hutton. You guys truly are Fantastically Great women! I wish you all the joy and greatness in your future work. The series would not have been the same without you guys.

To the super clever designers Katie Knutton and Peter Clayman – a big cheer for making the whole package look so beautiful ... and for dropping approximately 702 illustrations and doodles into layouts! Big thank you to Emily Ball, my new editor who has joined this project and helped it to sparkle and to Lotte Dobson for her amazing fact-checking skills.

This book is jam packed with amazing facts and examples of artwork – a massive thank you all the thoughtful research and writing Kate Paice did to make the book so intriguing, diverse and emotive.

It's all very well making a fascinating new book, but without the team in publicity and marketing not many people would know it existed! Massive round of applause to Emily Marples, Jade Westwood, Grace Ball and the rest of the Bloomsbury team for shouting very loudly about the books. And for looking after me so well as I travel around talking Fantastically Great Women to children at events.

Without my amazing agents, Hannah Whitty and Mark Mills, and the rest of the Plum Pudding team this series wouldn't have happened at all. Thank you for everything you guys have done for my career. I feel very fortunate for all the amazing experiences I've had working on this series.

Kate

We can all make our
wildest dreams come true. And the
**FANTASTICALLY GREAT WOMEN
SCIENTISTS**
in this book prove that women
can do anything.

Astronaut **MAE JEMISON'S** ambition was
out of this world. Brave volcanologist
KATIA KRAFFT wasn't afraid of fire.
CAROLINE HERSCHEL was never allowed
to be the star, but when she discovered
astronomy she began to shine.

Be inspired by their epic adventures
and life-changing discoveries. You have
the power to change the world too.

**What do YOU
dream of?**

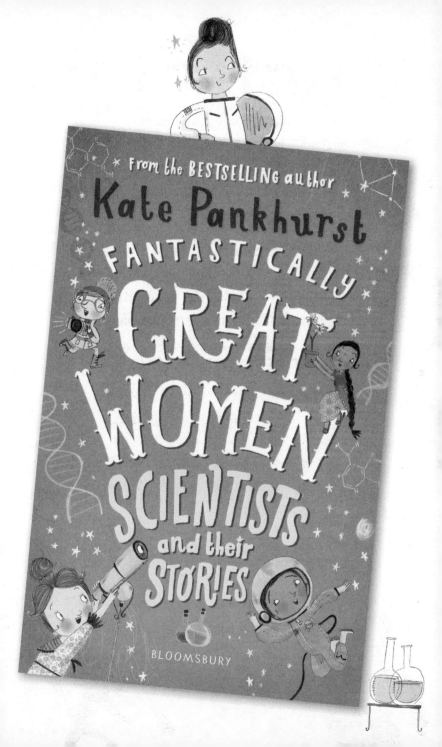

Also by
Kate Pankhurst

*Fantastically
Great Women
Who Changed
the World*

*Fantastically
Great Women
Who Made
History*

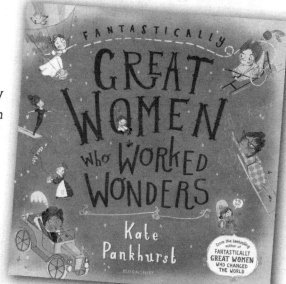

Fantastically Great Women Who Worked Wonders

Fantastically Great Women Who Saved the Planet

Available from www.bloomsbury.com

ABOUT THE AUTHOR

KATE PANKHURST is the bestselling author and illustrator of the trailblazing and internationally successful **FANTASTICALLY GREAT WOMEN** books. Kate's books have been translated into 22 languages and been shortlisted for many awards, including the NIBBIES award for Children's Illustrated and Non-fiction. Most recently, her first book, *Fantastically Great Women who Changed the World*, has been adapted into an inspiring stage show, touring the UK in 2021 and 2022.

Most days, Kate can be found illustrating and writing in her studio in Leeds with her spotty dog, Olive. She loves a good story, the funnier the better, and gets her best ideas by doodling in her sketchbook; because even quick, wonky drawings can spark ideas for amazing plots.